The Poetry of
R.S. Thomas

In Memory

Ronald Arthur Ward
Evelyn Annie Powell Ward

The Poetry of
R.S. Thomas

John Powell Ward

seren

seren is the book imprint of
Poetry Wales Press Ltd
Nolton Street, Bridgend, CF31 1EF, Wales
www.seren-books.com

ISBN 1-85411-252-X

A CIP record for this title is available from
the British Library

Cover photograph: Martin Roberts

*The publisher works with the financial assistance of the
Arts Council of Wales*

Printed in Plantin by CPD Wales, Ebbw Vale

Contents

Acknowledgements

The publisher is grateful to Orion Publishing and to Bloodaxe Books for permission to quote from the works of R.S. Thomas.

Preface: 1987 and 2000

For many people R.S. Thomas is one of the leading three or four religious poets of the twentieth century, its outstanding Welsh poet in English, and one of the ten or twenty of any kind in the language, British or otherwise, who will be remembered. Certainly it is hard to think of another who has followed his dark journey with such unflinching consistency and unforgettable metaphoric power. In his later years his work still evinced what it had always contained; a strong character covering a deep hurt, a piercing visual perception, the sharpest intelligence, and a profound longing for a gap to be filled. That all this does not dispel one's sense of a love and tenderness at the heart, further indicates his poetry's strength and intensity. His familiarity with the natural world was itself utterly natural, indeed increasingly strange to postmodern readers for whom the planet is no longer a process but a project, less a terrain than a convenience. Thomas's search for what for convenience he called God, seems curiously less strange. But it was no less consistent, and as a search rings no less true.

R.S. Thomas was born in Cardiff in 1913, but after an infancy on the move in England and Wales he spent childhood and youth in Holyhead in Anglesey. He then read Classics at the University of Wales, Bangor. His father was a merchant seaman and his mother the ward of an Anglican rector. He spoke at times with sadness if not bitterness about his (urban) place of birth, and made no secret of a certain antipathy toward his mother, deeply it seems because, by that parentage, he was deprived of Welsh as a first language. Yet he came to read and speak Welsh fluently although his medium of verse was English.

After his theological training Thomas entered the priesthood of the Church in Wales. His adult life was spent by choice close to nature, in or near rural villages in Wales. At first, at Manafon in Montgomeryshire, he tried to practise a pastoral vocation with low-paid agricultural workers and hill farmers, but found it hard going and the church's influence anyway in steep decline. The move to the more middle-class and retirement parish of Eglwysfach in Cardiganshire, with its notable proportion of English incomers, did not alter this impression. After a period of some inner conflict Thomas entered in the end on a sustained theological and indeed mystical quest, which became the subject of a group of books in the middle of his poetic career and which, in the very latest years, continued to be a central preoccupation. This preoccupation was flanked, on the one hand, by vociferous political campaigning for Wales, both its political independence and the centrality of the Welsh language to every aspect of life. Some of Thomas's most acerbic pronouncements were directed against "the English" as colonialist, tourist, or speaker of a foreign tongue. Equally acid, though, was his attitude to those Welsh who in his view had no stomach for the struggle and lay down under this intrusion.

The other dimension was ornithology. A twitcher's leisure-pursuit to some, the importance of birds in Thomas's imaginative life and his sense of the natural world we inhabit could hardly be exaggerated. Thomas's curt contempt for the technological trash which increasingly disfigures urban and rural life and indeed the remotest parts of the land's surface, lay in stark contrast to the winged creatures that soar freely in the empty space above it. Moorland and coast were also profound satisfactions and needs. Thomas was a bit more gregarious than has sometimes been acknowledged, but spending hours in long solitary walks in the country or on the seashore was always part of his life and basic to his poetry. His interests in philosophy, science, theology, painting and music also mark all his work. In 1967 Thomas moved to Aberdaron on the Lleyn peninsula where, again, new aspects of his poetic vision emerged. When his wife, the artist Mildred Elsi Eldridge, died in 1991 Thomas returned to the Anglesey of his youth. He married again in 1996, and died in September 2000.

Thomas's poetry can be seen as falling into five main periods. Each contains three collections of poetry, except the last which produced five. The early work dwelt vividly and tangibly on the Welsh hill landscape and peasantry, and was followed by a period of some indecision and self-questioning. There is then a clear new start with *H'm* (1972), and an equally well-defined new departure later still, with the group of poems about paintings which begins *Between Here and Now*, published in 1981. The final phase begins with *Experimenting with an Amen* (1986). That title itself suggests that collections from then on were aware of finality. Each is based on a self-contained conception, yet all Thomas's lifelong concerns remain, as though gathering each time for a last articulation. From time to time, also, there is a special sense that these five groupings stemmed from Thomas's five places or periods of residence in his adult years, even if the resulting work was sometimes long in the incubation. These periods were Manafon (1942-54), Eglwysfach (1954-67), Aberdaron as rector (1967-78), Aberdaron in retirement (1978-93), and finally Anglesey and elsewhere. However, this notion of residence raises rather a lot of questions; the thematic divisions, too, are bound to be approximations. The "long absorption with the plough" modulates into the galactic concerns with space only gradually, just as, in hindsight, one sees the interest in painting there all along with the wider visual orientations. Even so, these five divisions and periods lie, if generally, behind the present book's five main chapters. I continue to feel this is justified and hope it will commend itself accordingly.

In what follows, I have referred to the poet's sources as and when seemed necessary. There is no sustained attempt to identify or rank them consistently. R.S. Thomas absorbed his influences and covered his tracks with great skill, yet his critics have begun to identify quite a lot in recent years, in the Welsh tradition as much as the English, and will no doubt continue to do so. However, the pattern of main sources from mainstream English literature and traditional philosophy has been fairly constant even while emphases have fluctuated within that. There is the obvious background of the Bible, Plato, Shakespeare, the Anglican liturgy and the canon of Welsh history and literature. I continue to feel that Herbert, Milton, Yeats, Eliot and Stevens are the most important poets, and among the philosophers Kant, Coleridge, Nietzsche, Kierkegaard and Bergson; Wittgenstein joins the latter list in the later collections. Wordsworth too, of course, is an enormous influence, both as to his poetry and in his feeling for nature. Yet Wordsworth's way of taking nature into himself as his own meditation leaves it a little different from Thomas's nature, where item after item becomes symbolical, if not sacramental.

Thomas doesn't always refer to these sources explicitly. It happens on occasion, for example with Wittgenstein and Wallace Stevens in the later years. But it is better to say that these writers, more than others, form the climate in which Thomas's poetic apprehension occurs. The other major influence is the Welsh language and its literature. Here the present writer has competence to speak only in bare outline, and I say that fully aware that from the Welsh viewpoint the omission may seem a disabling one. As a poet writing in a language not his first choice, Thomas's position must be very rare, and it has its own enigmas within it. Sometimes he seems to have chosen English for its undeniable literary power; at others because needs must. A full-scale research study of Thomas's relation to the two languages and literatures would be as welcome as would one on his attitudes to nature and science. The same considerations apply to the church. I have tried to include basic information for readers outside Wales or the church, while not I hope being too tediously elementary for anyone already well-equipped in those areas.

However, the present book was first published thirteen years ago. There were sizeable developments in the intervening years, both as to R.S. Thomas himself and in the amount of critical response to his life and work. In 1987 one could state that "what has been written so far [about R.S. Thomas] is almost invariably brief...there are no full-length books". Since then critical reaction to R.S. Thomas has settled itself and become articulated. There have been at least three more critical books, and the avalanche of new essays has appeared more than once in the form of collections, which gives them a critical solidity. But Thomas himself also produced four more collections of poetry in this final period, so the 1987 edition of the present work had to be extended. There was therefore a danger of adding a chapter which explicitly engaged with this new criticism, to four earlier chapters written before such criticism existed. The only realistic approach was to write the new chapter in much the same vein as the earlier ones, and that is what I have done. I respect and have learnt greatly from much of this new material (notably work by Jason Walford Davies, M. Wynn Thomas and Barbara Prys Williams), and I hope its presence is there, if somewhat subliminally, in what I have added. The main new critical texts appear in the revised Bibliography. For similar reasons a full academic apparatus of references and footnotes is still omitted, as it was in the book's first edition in 1987; and it can only be hoped, even so, that the present edition will still provide whatever usefulness the first did. All that any of us says at this time will need revision, one would think, when the whole oeuvre is something like established in its full textual precision, as it presumably will be one day in the future.

The other matter is biography, and this is a more complex issue. There is currently a reaction, in literary criticism generally, against the biographical and historicist modes of the last two or three decades. In particular, aesthetic orientations have reasserted themselves, however widely they are defined. Yet many readers have also become distinctly more aware of R.S. Thomas's own life in the last decade. Formerly, for those outside his immediate circle, a certain mystique prevailed, but this later changed. Thomas's own much more frequent public appearances and utterances, his increasing eminence nationally and internationally (culminating in the nomination for the Nobel prize in 1996), the relentless researches of at least one English journalist, and finally the translation into English of his autobiographies in 1997 – all this made the figure behind the poetry far more visible in his final years, in something close to a factual profile. There are numerous recorded incidents, details of childhood, youth, and theological training, political involvement in well-authenticated events, and new testimonies from acquaintances. Thomas himself responded to this. His notoriously terse and sardonic remarks about both Wales and England received wide publicity but *The Echoes Return Slow*, in particular, also has a sense of his own life-events as deeply formative, not merely of the poetry generally, but of the occasions and even the meaning of actual poems, and the real people or places they refer to.

In 1987 I expressed a reluctance to write a critical biography of R.S. Thomas. Today this is hardly adequate as it stands, for once facts are known they can't be ignored, and the measure of their relevance to the resulting poetry has to be taken. At the same time – for reasons given below – one can still argue the case for directly textual studies of literary works, which is the mode in which this present book was originally conceived. As a result the text of the first four chapters and the book's overall ambience has been more or less retained, but with certain local adjustments. Where a shift of poetic tone comes with a change of parish and scenery or other new circumstance, that has now been alluded to, albeit briefly. Equally, in his autobiographies (see Bibliography) Thomas often refers to a particular matter with much the same imagery as he uses in poems of the time. This too has been noted. The new (fifth) chapter has been written in much the same way. The matter of biography is particularly discussed in context of *The Echoes Return Slow* (pages 155-158 below).

Indeed, Thomas's main autobiographies should be briefly referred to here. *No-one* (1985) and *A Year in Llyn* (1990) are an important complementary pair. The first has the stretch of an entire life, the second a single year. But this is to oversimplify, for the full

autobiography, while necessarily thinner, is never shallow, and the
purportedly single year in Llyn is clearly and sometimes explicitly a
composite of many years and seasons. *No-one* evinces a deep and
rich personality, in its range of tiny details and reflections on them.
"In the evening he would visit his parishioners, walking across the
fields toward some spot of light from the window, like a yellow flower
on the hillside". "R.S. was never fond of hymns, third-class verses
set to similar music." Of his deaf father: "it was a great pain for R.S.
to see him with his ear to the radio trying to hear the music" (pages
55, 83, 82). Yet the narration by the third-person "no-one" cuts
elliptically across such texture, leaving us wondering, not whether it
is true, but rather by what degrees of feeling and memory each truth
is clearer to us in each case. In *A Year in Llyn* the speaking personality is both submerged in and revealed by the different voice of the
professional observer of weather, terrain and wild-life daily witnessed. "There is a tendency to go over the top about an adder's
bite. Certainly, no one dies from it. It depends to some degree on
your age and your health. It depends also on the size of the snake
and the time that has elapsed since it last bit. The only thing that is
agreed upon is that it is exceedingly painful" (page 135). We see the
poet living hour by hour; the matter of nature is the pervading motif,
yet these minute events are interspersed with observations of people
and current news-items, and by wider philosophical and human gen-
eralisations which cover many years, not just one.

Yet there is another side to this debate. The profoundly reduc-
tive nature of some historicist criticism has been increasingly
recognized in recent years. It silently converts the poem into a prose
version of itself, and then uses the result as evidence about the poet's
beliefs or mode of living. The reaction against fully-fledged historicist criticism has followed from this. We can't expand this debate
here at length. But there are objections to a wholly biographical
approach – quite aside from the need for technical examination of
striking metaphor, powerful rhythm, tone and shape to which historicist criticism often adds little.

For example the resulting poem, placed next to the incident or
attitude from which it quite probably emanated, often feels all the
more different from it, rather than similar. Prose observations like
those cited above from *No-one* and *A Year in Llyn* are not inconsistent with Thomas's poetry. But in the poems they seem to have
moved across into another, strangely lit world of their own. Justin

Wintle's book is highly readable, but his class-reading of 'The Small Window' is to me dangerously one-dimensional. Certainly that poem's last few lines can be read as disdainful, but equally they may be wholly ironic. The result is a poem which bears both meanings at once, and so is spoken by language itself, by the very possibility of metaphoric articulation. A poet's experiences mingle in his and her darkness with the language of ancient centuries, infant glimpses of a world still enormous, half-remembered glories or nightmares, and numerous other things, in an alchemy which has little respect for what, in the event, actually "happened" that ostensibly led to the poem's creation.

Equally, readers do not always need to know a poet's life to get either the poem's immediate power or its universal bearing. The composer Paul Spicer has recorded this experience, relevantly to the present context. After a sonata of his had been premiered by the pianist Margaret Fingerhut at the Wigmore Hall in London, she invited him to write another work for her use. Fingerhut played the resulting work at the Three Choirs Festival in Gloucester in 1998. Spicer's programme-note on this composition's origin reads as follows: "Almost immediately I knew I wanted to write a piece based on the extraordinary Welsh priest/poet R.S. Thomas. I had come across Thomas's poetry quite by accident and I fell immediately for his vivid imagery; his wonderfully humanistic approach to religion; his acceptance of human weakness and its possibilities for redemption; and, most important of all, his feeling that time is of no importance." In personal communication to myself Paul Spicer has confirmed that, at the time of composition, he had virtually no knowledge of Thomas's personal or parish life whatsoever. Of course this leaves the political dimension in Thomas missing, but Spicer's very human reactions seem to have engaged with something that has floated clear of its origins. All this is supported by common experience. Monthly or weekly in contemporary journals and magazines we read and are often moved by new poems by poets we have never heard of. If we had to know their biographies to feel the figurative or human power of their work their careers would never leave the ground. So we have to be both guarded and subtle, it would seem, in taking the measure of a poem when we do know, even fairly accurately, something about when and where it was written.

As well as these two developments – of new critical responses to R.S. Thomas and of the criticism/biography debate generally – a third area could have been that of advances in the natural sciences in recent years. Thomas's preoccupation with science in our cultural and spiritual predicaments is well established, and in his final period he continued to respond to new technological in-puts and to some extent updates in pure theory. But the themes which had attracted public attention a decade earlier, then settled into place. These were the environment; cosmic origins; and the continuing implications of Darwinism as natural selection. Richard Dawkins's views on religion remain forceful, but they have received strong counter-attack and the debate continues. Pollution, population and global warming are standard issues – always present but no longer news – while any prospect of serious space-travel has declined for the foreseeable future. Our continuity with the animal kingdom and matter itself is hardly in dispute.

Rather, the pressure-points in natural science in the 1990s most concerned the human brain and body. Key areas included consciousness-theory and the detailed structure of the human genome. What seems so present to the individual as mind, emotion or attitude – long matters of importance to Thomas – could be taken down to the level of our gene-resources and the patterns of the multi-billion cells in our neural structures. But both these areas impinged largely after Thomas's latest four collections of poetry were published. Daniel Dennett's classic text *Consciousness Explained* – not that everyone thinks he explained it – didn't appear until 1991 (and in Britain a year later); later than all Thomas's published poetry up to *Mass for Hard Times*. Much-publicised work, as by Susan Greenfield and Susan Blackmore, came later still, and relevant philosophers like Thomas Nagel were not well known in Britain outside specialist circles. Consciousness was long held to be the last unsolved human mystery – in spiritual context, one might say, the last available locus for the human soul. But Thomas was never an explicitly soul-salvation poet. His orientations were always to do with the universe's origins; science's responsibility for good and evil; and the mystical listening for the godhead and poetic expression of its perennial elusiveness. In the words of *No-one* (Welsh *Neb*), "trying to plumb the mysteries of the creation", for "Who is it that ever saw God? Who ever heard him speak?" (pages 106, 104). As to the genome, its outcomes in genetic engineering are only now opening up before us.

Where a poem is quoted, I have usually only named the book where it appears if it falls outside the period under discussion, or if, as does happen with Thomas, the poem's title is used more than once in the period. This matter of Thomas's titles should be mentioned. He frequently re-uses a title, or one so similar as to be easily confused; for example 'A Labourer'/'The Labourer'; 'Arriving'/'Arrival'; 'Which'/'Which?' Well over sixty titles are implicated. Along with Thomas's curious one-word adverbial or pronominative titles – Once, Here, He, So, Other, Thus, This, That, Then, There, They, Again, Aside, No, Now, Ah! Who? and the rest, the danger of misidentification grows markedly. The tendency declines in the fifth period but is still there. Other titles name places, natural creatures or people ordinarily enough; yet one senses that the title is a soft lead-in for Thomas rather than a call for attention or a declaration of intent. But ordinary reader and professional scholar alike need to be watchful.

There is an Appendix on Thomas's half-dozen briefer collections. The present Preface has been rewritten but incorporates *en bloc* much of what was said first time round: hence the double-dating of its title. At my own invitation in 1987 R.S. Thomas read the original book after it was published and sent me a few brief comments. That however is the extent of his involvement, and he had no responsibility whatsoever – except in being its subject – for anything in either the first version or the present one. In our sporadic acquaintance over the years he was invariably kind and courteous, and never the purveyor of terse dismissals that one part of his reputation has commonly emphasized. As for my personal regard for R.S. Thomas's work and (as I understand it) his way of life, this present sentence will be the first and last mention of that; I can only trust that the following text conveys it adequately by implication. Expressing fully here my debt to Cary Archard and Mick Felton of Seren would be equally impossible — for commissioning the book in the first place, carrying through both editions, and their long-standing and constant wider friendship and support. I also owe an apology to the American critic Ted Cohen for originally attributing (in Chapter 1) a phrase of his to Paul Ricoeur; and I would like to thank Paul Spicer for permission to quote from his programme note above. The original book was dedicated to my mother and in memory of my father; with the passing of time it has now to be in memory of them both, but in gratitude, as before, for the combination of religion, liberality and nature they always held out to me.

John Powell Ward, October 2000

Of that Forbidden Tree, whose mortal tast
Brought death into the world, and all our woe,
With loss of Eden
                              – John Milton

I love the great despisers because they are also the great adorers,
arrows of longing for the further shore.   – Friedrich Nietzsche

Then take my hand that is
of the bone the island
is made of, and looking at
me say what time it is
on love's face, for we have
no business here other than
to disprove certainties the clock knows.

                                        – R.S. Thomas

I. The Figure Rooted

(*Song at the Year's Turning* 1955, *Poetry for Supper* 1958,
Tares 1961)

In one of R.S. Thomas's best known early poems, 'Affinity', the first line reads, "Consider this man in the field beneath". It is characteristic of the approach and setting of a number of poems in *Song at the Year's Turning*, the book from which it comes. This book includes some poems already published in two earlier locally printed works *The Stones of the Field* (1946) and *An Acre of Land* (1952), and is one of Thomas's two or three longest collections. The fact that it did not appear until 1955 shows us how long it was in the gestation and for how much of his early adult life Thomas was absorbed in the book's material and themes.

The collection contains a great many poems on the Welsh peasant and hill farmer. The peasant is commonly seen in the same way. He is alone. He is in a field. He is watched by the poet and, as "beneath" suggests, from a raised position some way away, with a tinge of social distance implied as well. There is no physical contact between the priest and the usually solitary member of his flock; so much so, that we have to remind ourselves of the cordial handshake or arm round the shoulder which might in other circumstances, and between different people, have been in evidence. The poet is not detached emotionally, but is certainly distant. This cultural gap is alluded to also in 'A Priest to His People' ("I have taxed your ignorance of rhyme and sonnet") and is very present in the poet's tone of voice. It is slightly strained and somewhat unrelenting. Furthermore the voice usually does not speak to the peasant but to the reader, or is overheard in soliloquy. The peasant appears to be a case for consideration, compassion or conscience. Here is 'A Labourer':

> Who can tell his years, for the winds have stretched
> So tight the skin on the bare racks of bone
> That his face is smooth, inscrutable as stone?

And when he wades in the brown bilge of earth
Hour by hour, or stoops to pull
The reluctant swedes, who can read the look
In the colourless eye, as his back comes straight
Like an old tree lightened of the snow's weight?
Is there love there, or hope, or any thought
For the frail form broken beneath his tread,
And the sweet pregnancy that yields his bread?

There are some exceptions to this general description. In 'Death of a Peasant' and 'Evans' the peasant is in bed dying. In 'Memories' and 'Valediction' the farmer is addressed, as of course is Prytherch in the group of poems which soon come to surround that imaginary character. In 'The Hill Farmer Speaks' and 'Invasion on the Farm' the peasant himself speaks in the first person. But the image we take away from reading these poems is that of the priest watching, even staring, at a lone worker in a field and trying to make something of what he sees, which evidently absorbs him repeatedly. The priest is not introverted, and we are given no details of the priest himself. The priest offers no help with the job, never enquires after the family and most notably sees these peasants and farmers one at a time. It may be said that the hill farmer was solitary as a matter of fact. Yet some poems such as 'Out of the Hills' and 'Meet the Family' contain matter the poet could have employed much more often if he had wanted to render familial or communal life. It is not that we blame the poet for these omissions. R.S. Thomas's solitary peasant would appear to have a deeper origin in the poet's own culture and emotions, and the peasant has a curious luminosity as a result.

Many of these very early presentations of the peasant begin with this act of seeing. "Consider this man in the field beneath" ('Affinity'), "That man, Prytherch, with the torn cap,/I saw him often" ('The Gap in the Hedge'), "Ah, you should see Cynddylan on a tractor" ('Cynddylan on a Tractor'), "A man is in the fields, let us look with his eyes" ('Enigma'), "Look at this village boy" ('Farm Child'), "There he goes, tacking against the fields'/Uneasy tides" ('The Labourer'), and finally from the first book as though the theme is at least temporarily exhausted, "A man, a field, silence – what is there to say?" ('Autumn on the Land'). From these cases, every one of which is a poem's opening line, it slowly becomes clear that the poet's compulsive staring is of considerable significance.

As a young parish priest at Manafon, Thomas found that his flock consisted of many people of whom he could make nothing, and for which his own theological training had hardly prepared him. He attested to this outside his poetry. He had, at first, an idealistic expectation; but the hope that the hill farmer had a nobility drawn from nature itself, or might even appreciate the church and its liturgy and arts, relentlessly subsided. As a result the poet was left to tease out the enigma behind the "inscrutable gaze" he confronted. He stared, and they stared back.

At first the poet tried to speak with the ringing tones of the preacher. This occurs most obviously in 'A Priest to His People', but is not confined to that poem. At the beginning of the book, more generally, the poet's speech is not inhibited, and by Thomas's own later and invariably astringent standards not especially economic. The first poem, 'Out of the Hills', offers a speculative and unusually full picture of a peasant not only on the land but going to the town and the pub in the evening where one presumes the poet did not accompany him. It is fulsomely written, words are not wasted, yet there is not yet the terseness so characteristic of this poet in later years. In 'A Peasant', a poem often quoted, the poet engages with his subject through a range of vivid details authoritatively offered. These however turn out to work on different and conflicting levels. The peasant is closely seen rooted down in the muck

> Docking mangels, chipping the green skin
> From the yellow bones with a half-witted grin
> Of satisfaction, or churning the crude earth
> To a stiff sea of clods that glint in the wind –

and we feel only a hint, hardly noticed, of the clipped punning to such ironic and bitter effect (here in "clods") which Thomas will employ again and again in the books to come. At home the peasant "leans to gob in the fire", and the first uncompromising facing of what has to be faced follows:

> There is something frightening in the vacancy of his mind.

Yet there is more than this. This same sweaty figure who grins and spits, also "pens a few sheep in a gap of cloud". It is this surprising contrast of the down-to-earth and the etherealized that becomes "your prototype", and we are left with an equally formal but serious concluding injunction:

> Remember him, then, for he, too, is a winner of wars,
> Enduring like a tree under the curious stars.

That is to say, the stars as well as the priest are watching. The
priest's staring may begin as a psychic compulsion, but it ends as
something romanticized and sublime in the natural world. This is a
remarkable picture, for the adjective "curious" may be taken in
either direction. The picture of the peasant rooted where the centuries have held him, under the watching stars which equally are
curious objects, suggests that the "prototype" the poet has found has
become part of a natural tableau of cosmic significance. It is in this
same poem 'A Peasant' that the general term "prototype" is used.

But in late twentieth century terms, being watched by the con-
stellations is hardly recompense for so much muck and toil. In
'Affinity' the implication at first seems more obviously social.
Although the poet as usual invites us to look, or draws us into his
own looking, we have no detailed description of the peasant such as
'A Peasant' gave and as so many of the other poems about the farmers also give. Instead we have a challenging question:

> From the standpoint of education or caste or creed
> Is there anything to show that your essential need
> Is less than his, who has the world for church
> And stands bare-headed in the woods' wide porch
> Morning and evening to hear God's choir
> Scatter their praises?

This seems an egalitarian question with which the poet is faced. And
yet, as in the earlier poem, again the answer is not of that kind.
Again the poet reaches out for some way of lodging the peasant's
figure in our consciousness by tying it to the large and permanent
features in nature. Again the symbol is in the heavens:

> He also is human, and the same small star,
> That lights you homeward, has inflamed his mind
> With the old hunger, born of his kind.

Thirty or forty years on, it might seem a conventional romantic
flourish. But either way it is the symbol, not the social inference

alone, that endures, and the questions and their accompanying loud and wordy bewilderment that gradually subside.

The same is true of the poem 'A Priest to His People'. Here the poet releases his pulpit power at the peasants directly, and throws lucid descriptions and earthy tangible metaphors at them, so that, even in recognising how little he understands them, he still seems to take on himself the authority to do all the talking. The poem begins with a kind of friends-Romans-countrymen gesture ("Men of the hills, wantoners, men of Wales"), outlines "all the devices of church and school" and the fine and literary arts too, as well as the failure of those things to get any response from the suspicious congregation. He even instructs his people how to respond:

> You will forgive, then, my initial hatred,
> My first intolerance of your uncouth ways

And of course the educated clergyman did still retain some authority in the middle of this century, certainly in rural areas. And yet in this poem the outcome is still just the same as before. The poet cannot avoid the symbolic attachment. The peasants will go on living

> In a crude tapestry under the jealous heavens
> To affront, bewilder, yet compel my gaze.

The voice of the preacher leaves R.S. Thomas's poetry quite early, in fact well before the end of the first section of this book. But the compulsion to watch the peasant in a gap of cloud, under the sky, under the stars, does not. Rather, it is that prototype of the single peasant that endures, and seems gradually to appear from the scenery , the miscellaneous other hill people, old women, children, figures from Welsh history, and others, and be put into a strange, lasting light. We see this very clearly in the poem 'Soil' which has the usual subject, but a different tone:

> A field with tall hedges and a young
> Moon in the branches and one star
> Declining westward set the scene
> Where he works slowly astride the rows
> Of red mangolds and green swedes
> Plying mechanically his cold blade.

> This is his world, the hedge defines
> The mind's limits; only the sky
> Is boundless and he never looks up;
> His gaze is deep in the dark soil,
> As are his feet. The soil is all;
> His hands fondle it, and his bones
> Are formed out of it with the swedes.
> And if sometimes the knife errs,
> Burying itself in his shocked flesh,
> Then out of the wound the blood seeps home
> To the warm soil from which it came.

The scene is suffused with an eerie lunar light. It is static, as in a dream. The absence of punctuation and strong main verb in the first stanza enforces these qualities; as does the bare contrast of "red mangolds and green swedes", as though some pure palette from nature's elements is being used to depict the setting. The preacher's voice has wholly gone. Indeed the stanza seems to be thought rather than said. Yet these same features enable the poet to probe the peasant's condition from a new and surprising perspective. The hedge defines the mind's limits; and so the sky against which Prytherch had earlier been seen cannot entice the peasant into thinking, despite that it alone has the quality of infinity in which the more philosophical mind can find fulfilment. The peasant is awakened to attention only when his flesh is damaged. The latent hint of sexuality, which will come into the open throughout the poetry later until it finally arranges itself round the Garden of Eden story, does not here tempt the peasant's mind into any kind of knowledge. The peasant's hands fondle only the soil, and if he was formed out of it as Adam was out of dust, it makes him only into a vegetable.

And in this respect he is, certainly, analogous to the tree that was "enduring...under the curious stars" in the earlier poem. The peasant as tree had appeared in other poems too; for example in 'A Labourer' which we quoted, where "as his back comes straight" he is "like an old tree lightened of the snow's weight", a brilliant image characteristic of the driving force of Thomas's poetic power. In 'Peasant Greeting' the silently raised hand had signalled "the land's patience and a tree's/Knotted endurance". There the double meaning of "knotted" twists some feeling of neurosis into the farmer's stoical acceptance. And in 'An Old Man' (*Song at the Year's Turning*) the poet sees, not merely a comparison, but a common organic feature:

Looking upon this tree with its quaint pretension
Of holding the earth, a leveret, in its claws...
I understand whence this man's body comes

So the peasant survives as the tree or plant in the dark soil under the sky or stars, and this is where the poet's compulsion has taken him. The image of the tree as both source and limit of knowledge, and locus of sacrifice too, is ubiquitous in Thomas's poetry from here on.

There is of course more to be said. But it seems to me that this gradual gathering of his observations of the farmer in the field on many occasions into one luminous figure, is what gave rise to Thomas's creation, Iago Prytherch, about whom so much has been written. The peasant "compels" the poet's gaze, yet compulsion psychically is subjective. It is the necessary correlative, or the archetypal Other, that the Protestant religious mystic has to generate; it is the revolutionary's ideological opponent, the focus of the neurotic lover's double-bind and the entrepreneur's obsessive focus of financial ambition. Years later Thomas will stare into pools and mirrors, at God or the gap where God ought to be, and at painting after painting on the walls of the Louvre. This single-mindedness is the logical outcome for the individual versed in a tradition like Protestantism, which makes the inner conscience more important than other thoughts or feelings; and this single-mindedness needs to focus itself on some external entity to avoid an inner life which constantly self-circles. From this comes the further tendency not merely to homogenize the many figures of the landscape into one, but also to address that figure. God is not addressed at all in this first book, and (although his presence hovers increasingly) is hardly addressed at all in this first period before the end of *Tares*.

Thomas the young clergyman is straining to reach across to the farm workers among whom he lives. Yet the remarkable thing about Prytherch is that he is so elusive. It is as though his name was brought in (and R.S. Thomas stated outside his poetry how this came about), but one which then stayed as a magnet for this particular kind of attention. Prytherch appears only five times in the sixty-odd poems in *Song at the Year's Turning*, and in most of these the insertion of the name does not make what is then said differ in any material way from what is said of other, unnamed farmers. After the systematic description in 'A Peasant' (the "prototype...enduring

like a tree under the curious stars"), Prytherch is addressed in two
poems, 'Memories' and 'Lament for Prytherch'; he himself speaks
throughout one, 'Invasion on the Farm', but most intriguingly is also
elusively seen under translucent light in 'The Gap in the Hedge':

> That man, Prytherch, with the torn cap,
> I saw him often, framed in the gap
> Between two hazels with his sharp eyes,
> Bright as thorns, watching the sunrise...

Is it just possible to see R.S. Thomas here hovering on the edge
of a crucifixion scene, with Prytherch in the "gap" that for years in
a later period God is going to have vacated? The peasant is
"between two hazels", perhaps thieves crucified, and a crown of
"thorns" can at least enter our consciousnesses. At the end of the
poem with its Yeatsian echo there is, equally, a touch of suggestion
of Easter morning:

> For he's still there
> At early morning, when the light is right
> And I look up suddenly at a bird's flight.

The point is, that Prytherch's own persona constantly changes,
constantly eludes. Sometimes he is rarified and ethereal, as here, but
sometimes he is down in the mixen "sour with years of sweat" and
satisfied with his "half-witted grin". Sometimes he is an ordinary
farmer, ignorant and nervous: "I am Prytherch. Forgive me. I don't
know/What you are talking about"; yet sometimes he is just imagin-
ably a companion for Immanuel Kant himself, as in 'Green
Categories'. Sometimes he is the peasant piercingly attacked for his
loutish and uncouth stupidity, as 'Absolution' in hindsight recognizes, and yet sometimes the priest is the one who understands and
knows where others do not:

> They see you as they see you,
> A poor farmer with no name,
> Ploughing cloudward, sowing the wind
> With squalls of gulls at the day's end.
> To me you are Prytherch, the man
> Who more than all directed my slow
> Charity where there was need.
>   ('The Dark Well')

In these last two cases it may be answered that a merely temporal change has occurred, and that the poet has come to understand the peasant's virtues after unthinkingly taunting him earlier. But later still, in 'Too Late' in *Tares*, it is Prytherch himself who has fallen to the lure of "the pound's whistle". I feel we have to conclude that the only consistency is the one already noted; the sublimated prototype "ploughing cloudward, sowing the wind", under the sky, that space which seems to release the poet's strongest metaphorical power.

The question of Prytherch is finally made explicit by the poet himself. It is found in two poems near the end of *Tares*, the second of these being 'Which?' Every sentence in the poem (not here given in full) is itself a question:

And Prytherch – was he a real man,
Rolling his pain day after day
Up life's hill? Was he a survival
Of a lost past, wearing the times'
Shabbier cast-offs, refusing to change
His lean horse for the quick tractor?
Or was a wish to have him so
Responsible for his frayed shape?

I think one can overstress the extent to which a poem must be read in the context of those which precede and follow it, as if only through them can meaning be fully found. The poem must be able to stand alone. Yet there is no doubt that R.S. Thomas ordered his collections in careful sequences, as did Yeats, one of Thomas's chief influences in this period particularly; and 'Which?' does seem closely connected to 'The Watcher' which comes right before it. For 'The Watcher' is about this compulsive staring itself, so that the start of 'Which?' then feels like the general watching applied to a particular case. The poet seems to ask, did I really see *him*, or was it just a projection of watching in general? In 'The Watcher' it is the watching itself that is finally grasped:

He was looking down on a field;
Not briefly, but for a long time.
A gate opened; it had done so before,
A sluice through which in a flood came
Cattle and sheep, occasionally men,
To fan out in a slow tide,
The stock to graze, the men busy

In ways never to be divulged
To the still watcher beyond the glass
Of their thin breath, the ear's membrane
Stretched in vain, for no words issued
To curse or bless through those teeth clenched
In a long grip on life's dry bone.

The poet's feeling for the farmers is intense. And yet the phrase at the centre, "in ways never to be divulged", sounds rather final. It is not merely a rueful surrendering. Though sad, its slow curved rhythm makes it feel firm. This is not at all to say that nothing can be changed, that no attempt to improve social conditions or alter values can be successful. R.S. Thomas was long active in the campaigns for an independent Wales, the survival of its language and for nuclear disarmament. It is rather that there is a deeper dimension, the unalterable constraints of planetary existence at all, that also are found uniquely in the constitution of any individual. And this poet finds that he, as individual and as poet, is a watcher; that he must watch, that this is the mode of his poetry and that this will not be changed.

Consequently, it seems that Prytherch is not a particular person, nor only a generalization of persons, the farmers and peasants among whom the priest-poet has lived and worked. Rather he is a drawing-out of the poet's other self, but through the mode of the others who most compel his gaze. This drawing out is found in Prytherch's true realization, I feel, as the one person the poet talks to. The priest can get no answer from the farmers at the level of sermon or ordinary talk ("You who are indifferent to all that I can offer"), yet they compel his gaze still. In some form he must make communication.

The result is found in the conversation poems, so to call them; 'Memories' from *Song at the Year's Turning* and 'Temptation of a Poet', 'Green Categories', 'Iago Prytherch' and 'Absolution' from *Poetry for Supper*. Apart from 'Too Late', which is a little sterner in any case, there is no poem of this kind in *Tares*. In these other five poems the theme is more universal. Very early on R.S. Thomas expressed the hope that Prytherch would be "the first man in the new community", but this is in a poem in *The Stones of the Field* which was not reprinted. The poet saw, surely, that the transcendent symbol and the social hope cannot be merged in that way. Instead, in all these five poems there is as it were the dialogue that would be, or would have been, if the peasant had been able to speak his patient age-old toil on the land, and if the poet had in some other existence been a peasant, had fusing through his own poet's personality the ignorance, dirt and stumbling inarticulacy themselves. Perhaps the poet-priest is expressing a yearning for the impossible. But this does not make it merely 'idealistic', or the poet rambling to himself through a hallucination. The poems are real, and without real peasants could not have been written. That, surely, is the significance of Iago Prytherch.

In 'Memories', the poet seems to long for this articulation of what he and the peasant shared in the past:

> Come, Iago, my friend, and let us stand together
> Now in the time of the mild weather...
>   ...and I will sing
> The land's praises, making articulate
> Your strong feelings, your thoughts of no date,
> Your secret learning, innocent of books.

It releases a cornucopia of astonishing metaphors:

> Do you remember the shoals of wheat, the look
> Of the prawned barley, and the hissing swarm
> Of winged oats busy about the warm
> Stalks? Or the music of the taut scythe
> Breaking in regular waves upon the lithe
> Limbs of the grass?

"Shoals", "swarm", "waves" – apart from the contrasting force the marine images give (and also incidentally "busy", one of Thomas's signature-words) it is the abundance and life which these plurals give that is compelling. It is as though the poet is saying, you have seen and known so much, if only you could say so; and the form, the rhetorical question, is a longing for the peasant to be able to answer: yes, that is exactly how it was. The poet has turned the Pauline rhetorical question of the traditional nonconformist pulpit to a different use. So great is his own word-power, that the priest can confidently project the affirmative answer: "Yes, though your lips are sealed/By a natural reticence, your eyes betray/ The heart's rich harvest..."

In 'Green Categories' there is a similar projection of the impossible but the real because created. In this poem Prytherch is imagined meeting the philosopher Kant. Again it is highly improbable (even if Kant were alive), but the result is compelling even so. Kant's pure logic would have been inadequate for a world where "things exist rooted in the flesh,/Stone, tree and flower", while Iago too would have stumbled in face of "the cold wind/Of genius". But the symbol of their rarefied union is one we have by now long come to expect from Thomas:

> ...you could have been at one,
> Sharing your faith over a star's blue fire.

We may feel in cold prose that any real Iago Prytherch would not remotely have understood such ideas. But that does not matter, for Thomas creates an alternative setting in which, by common humanity in an equally shared cosmos, the union could have occurred.

All the other three poems are as though from a later time when the poet looks back on the relationship now past. In 'Temptation of a Poet' it is acknowledged that poetry itself is what is desired, and culled, by that strange relationship; furthermore again, that "the lost poetry of our talk" is not mere relationship alone. Rather it is from the prior source of the natural world and self-generating:

> ...not built either,
> But found lingering on the farm
> As sun lingers about the corn
> That in the stackyard makes its own light.

And in the remaining two poems, by making explicit the rueful confession of his own taunting attitude to the peasant and his world when they were first encountered, the poet puts these remarkable invented dialogues into a world not only actual, but uncomfortable and regretted. In 'Iago Prytherch' the poet recalls how he "made fun of" the peasant, yet that the peasant too lived in rags and was irredeemably ignorant of culture and science. In 'Absolution', which I see as one of Thomas's most memorable poems, the ethereal prototype is established permanently.

> Prytherch, man, can you forgive
> From your stone altar on which the light's
> Bread is broken at dusk and dawn

One who strafed you with thin scorn
From the cheap gallery of his mind?
It was you who were right the whole time;
Right in this that the day's end
Finds you still in the same field
In which you started, your soul made strong
By the earth's incense, the wind's song.
While I have worn my soul bare
On the world's roads, seeking what lay
Too close for the mind's lenses to see,
And come now with the first stars
Big on my lids westward to find
With the slow uplifting of your hand
No welcome, only forgiveness.

Within a natural and sacramental setting the poet now finally faces the use he has made of the very man he is addressing. The terms are mythological and elemental, but the poet's belief that he needs forgiveness is far from imaginary. Iago was not only "right" but real, actually there in the field over the years, no matter what poetry was made from him or what the poet's own voice and compulsion to metaphor tried to say through the peasant or about him. The result is not, however, that the poet remains with Iago in a dull and "real" field after all, for that would suggest a disbelief in the poetry that has nonetheless resulted. Rather the continuing symbol still hovers overhead, as yet again the poet must

> come now with the first stars
> Big on my lids westward...

It seems, then, that there is a slowly emerging prototype in this first period, a lasting figure connected in its poetry to the permanent features of the natural world and cosmos. It is an extraordinary thing to have achieved and, in an age of social consciousness, to be left with. But one cannot leave it there, and the poet does not. The figure would not have been possible without the presence of the peasant in the actual uplands of central Wales, and in considerable deprivation. This is the different necessary dimension behind the ethereality that is achieved. This raises the matter of how Thomas depicts the peasant as suffering, working for a lifetime in deplorable conditions to get a tiny return out of bad soil; and also experiencing the crampedness of mind, the darkened and at times twisted emotions that result from such conditions. The prototype transcendent peasant is lifted up out of this and made worthwhile in some wider scheme of things. What he comes from, the scene of agricultural work and political Wales, remains.

For the peasant himself R.S. Thomas finds a rare, different voice:

> I am the farmer, stripped of love
> And thought and grace by the land's hardness;
> But what I am saying over the fields'
> Desolate acres, rough with dew,
> Is, Listen, listen, I am a man like you.

He ends:

> The tale of my life is smirched with dung;
> The phlegm rattles. But what I am saying
> Over the grasses rough with dew
> Is, Listen, listen, I am a man like you.
>   ('The Hill Farmer Speaks')

It is one of the very few cases where the farmer speaks in his own voice. The curious effect of non sequitur in this poem, "But what I am saying...", and the awkward rhythm, are extremely moving, and it is as if the inarticulate farmer has grasped hold of a single sentence which he knows expresses all that matters, and to which he desperately clings. Able to say nothing else, still this truth contains the only hope of relief from his plight, if only it could be heard. It is I feel the central poem of its theme in the first book, even though many others such as 'The Labourer', 'The Lonely Farmer', 'Autumn on the Land' and 'The Last of the Peasantry' give relentless pictures from the point of view of the distanced priest, staring as ever.

But, in these poems too, it is as if the peasant's plight is made all the more discomfited by being so stared at and so exposed. Under that cold light the farmers are caught in the act of being their wretched selves. "What do you see? Notice the twitching hands..." "What does he know? moving through the fields..." To say this is not to accuse the priest of lack of sensitivity. Rather the suggestion is that the peasants' condition, in every aspect, cannot be overlooked by anyone with greater cultivation and social privilege, never mind intelligence. Where the peasants are limited they suffer and endure, but their pain is also an offence to others. At the crudest level, they stink, of cow-dung and sweat. In terms of a fuller humanity they irritate, and their stupefied response to outsiders and to each other makes for impatience if not worse. This raises the matter of the profound tension in Thomas's poetry between his sympathy for the hill farmers and his equal condemnation of them. Again it raises the matter of political Wales.

One poem in *Poetry for Supper*, 'The Muck Farmer', gets as near as any to icy dismissal. Another, 'Evans', watches the peasant move toward an appalling and destitute death for which the poet feels compassion. But it is in *Tares* that this two-edged engagement with the peasant's lot is at its deepest and most uncompromising. The first and last poems in the book are on the two aspects. In the first poem, 'The Dark Well', it is the peasant's anguish that matters. The poet tries to share it, and tells

> the story of one whose hands
> Have bruised themselves on the locked doors
> Of life; whose heart, fuller than mine
> Of gulped tears, is the dark well
> From which to draw, drop after drop,
> The terrible poetry of his kind.

"Gulped" shows Thomas as near to exposing his compassion as anywhere. It is terrible, but poetry; it matters, and in hindsight we can feel that the transcendent prototype under the cosmic lights of night and day is the best, and only, recompense the poet can offer, for it is drawn most deeply out of his own self. But in the book's last poem, 'The Survivor', a very different picture is offered:

> The land's thug: seventeen stone,
> Settling down in a warm corner
> By a wood fire's lazy purr;
> A slumped bundle of fat and bone.

This man is eighty-five, his life of bragging and "pride and hate" nearly gone, and for which the remedy is terse and severe:

> Wake him up. It is too late
> Now for the blood's foolish dreaming...
> Old and weak, he must chew now
> The cud of prayer and be taught how
> From hard hearts huge tears are wrung.

The last line is a rare case, in modern poetry, of more than styl-
istic alliteration really working by reinforcing the emphasis. Between
these first and last poems in *Tares* we encounter the farmer many
times and in different shades. He is traced through wartime, where
the land itself is infected with the savagery of the war itself. In 'An
Old Man' an old man is walking in the winter and tries "time's
treacherous ice with a slow foot"; and in 'Hireling', the peasant with
no car is rendered hopeless by owning nothing. "Nothing is his, neither the land/Nor the land's flocks". There are other old men; there
is Walter Llywarch, "sure prey of the slow virus/ Bred in quarries of
grey rain".

But there is also a new self-questioning in the poet. This is
found in many poems in *Tares* and is a markedly new feature. And
it, too, has an inherent tension. In 'The Face', early in the book,
the poet faces that his clinical probing of the peasant was something
instinctive:

> I knew when
> I first saw him that was the man
> To turn the mind on, letting its beam
> Discover rottenness at the seams
> Of the light's garment I found him in.
>
> Did I look long enough or too long?

Later, in 'Those Others', the poet raises to consciousness his long
looking at, not now the peasant, but the land, now in the sense of
the nation, where the peasant belongs:

> I have looked long at this land,
> Trying to understand
> My place in it – why,
> With each fertile country
> So free of its room,
> This was the cramped womb
> At last took me in
> From the void of unbeing.

In both cases the poet looks, still looks, and this looking is a
mode from which R.S. Thomas will never depart. But the tension
to which we have referred, between the poet's compassion for the
peasant and his equally impatient contempt, finds an analogue in

another difficulty, whether the peasant's failings are his own or those of circumstance. It is not a simple parallel, and it is not enough to say that there is individual sin or shortcoming from the religious or personal viewpoint, and exploitation and political domination from another standpoint, making the same individual sometimes agent, sometimes victim. The shifts are more complex, there are grey areas and dark ones. It is the wretched and infertile soil, and the political history, that leave some communities to wrest their living out of such terrain while others are more fortunate, that nurtures seeds of bitter hatred and uncouth imbecility. But those then so take hold on the personality, that in the end it is idle to blame some external source for it, even if we still feel that is true. Hatred is hatred, mean-ness of mind is meanness of mind, and somehow one cannot "care" for ever, however harsh the circumstances that created such charac-teristics. This is the basis of the tension in which the poet finds himself. Thomas is aware that the vile emotions he sees in the dis-possessed can be infectious:

> Hate takes a long time
> To grow in, and mine
> Has increased from birth...
>   I find
> This hate's for my own kind,
> For men of the Welsh race...

It is a matter of focus. In the short poems where the farmer is stared out into the open, we feel that circumstances largely shaped him, even though the result is not attractive. But when the descrip-tion is extended, as in 'The Survivor' or the much longer poem 'The Airy Tomb', this makes the examined personality much more visible in its complexity. Its more twisted side seems much more its own responsibility. The same matter can be seen from the different angle of orthodox social science. On the one hand humanity is found in individuals' bodies and minds; and from there as with rip-ples spreading outward, there is encounter with the family, street or local community, wider occupational groups, class and finally soci-ety. But equally one may take it from the other end, and see 'society' as preceding and surviving any person and personal influ-ence, and the single person is then seen as constantly at the mercy of a flow of pressures, constraints and (for some) opportunities, which largely form personal identity. But there is a big gap between single individual and whole society, which it is very hard to see across. Despite his undoubted feeling that the condition and tradition and pride (or lack of it) of Wales is what causes the sad failings and crass limitations of the peasant farmer, Thomas's own immediate physical perception, his sharp vision and direct psychological penetration, seem always to have taken him back to the individual presently witnessed. This is true of his peasants, but also of the old women, young blondes, sailors and other people he encounters; and his engagement with Wales is thus at a different level.

From the start Thomas tried to write an Anglo-Welsh poetry based on the heritage of the real Wales. This resulted in the very consciously Welsh poems in the first book, such as 'Wales', 'The Rising of Glyndwr', 'Night and Morning', 'The Ancients of the World' and some others. 'Border Blues', the opening poem of *Poetry For Supper*, is an interesting piece of writing despite a too evident debt to Eliot's *The Waste Land*. 'On Hearing a Welshman Speak' and 'Expatriates' are terse, sharp pieces. But there are no other Welsh poems in that book. In *Tares* the issues are made more explicit than previously. But the poem 'A Welsh Testament' ends with its question unanswered ("Did the door open/To let me out or yourselves in?"), while in 'Hyddgen' the constant attempt to reinvigorate the Glyndwr story now yields only a fatigue:

> He beat the English.
> Does it matter now
> In the rain? The English
> Don't want to come...

In contrast to these attempts, it is surprisingly early in the first book that the note for Wales, both national and physically immediate, is sounded:

> To live in Wales is to be conscious
> At dusk of the spilled blood
> That went to the making of the wild sky,
> Dyeing the immaculate rivers
> In all their courses.
> It is to be aware,
> Above the noisy tractor
> And hum of the machine
> Or strife in the strung woods,

Vibrant with sped arrows.
You cannot live in the present,
At least not in Wales.
There is the language for instance,
The soft consonants
Strange to the ear.
There are cries in the dark at night
As owls answer the moon,
And thick ambush of shadows,
Hushed at the fields' corners.
There is no present in Wales,
And no future;
There is only the past,
Brittle with relics,
Wind-bitten towers and castles
With sham ghosts;
Mouldering quarries and mines;
And an impotent people,
Sick with inbreeding,
Worrying the carcase of an old song.

('Welsh Landscape')

A poem secures its permanent existence, not merely by saying,
but also by being what it says. But equally, it can do so by being not
what it says. This poem, which I feel is a great poem, is not what it
says. Evidently Wales does not exist merely in the past, for its living
presence and spirit throb on our pulses; "the spilled blood...dyeing
the immaculate rivers/In all their courses"..."strife in the strung
woods,/Vibrant with spent arrows". The trees themselves quiver
with triumphant warfare; the voice there is not of a loser, no matter
what the literal facts may be. And how can the language be dead
when it resonates so softly and with such interpenetration with the
noises of the night birds? Neither sham nor impotent, this Welsh
poet invests his metaphor with an anger which is to be its energizing spirit in figure after figure in the poems to come, "Worrying the
carcase of an old song". It is as though the distance of the comparison from the thing compared, is allowed by the defiance itself; the
tone in which the poet says, it's as bad as that, even *that* can be seen
in the same light as the things you are presuming to value. The key,
even the secret, is in the first line. It is not "To be Welsh", but topo-
graphically to live in Wales; that is what survives.

R.S. Thomas was seldom able to write of Wales in this vein

again, and seemingly did not try to. Perhaps because his perceptive
powers were so concrete, he tended towards aspects of the Welsh
predicament in the lives of people he wrote about immediately, and
visibly. In short, the exploiters and appropriators are not the English
politicians but the English tourists. (There are also the landowners
who are English or affiliate with them, but this is far rarer, as in
'Rhodri' in *Pietà* and 'Plas Difancoll' in *Later Poems*.) These tourists
bring their cars, litter, listless voices and cheap consumer goods to
the Welsh scene. But it is more than that. The matter is too complex, as was shown by the poet's earlier attempts to render formally
a history's lasting moments. The poem that really grasps the Wales
Thomas knew is 'The Minister'. With certain changes this poem
could have been set in other parts of Britain, although as it stands it
is inescapably of Wales. But it does not need to name its country,
any more than do *The Canterbury Tales* or *Tintern Abbey*, outside of
their titles. The scene and characters are already sizeable enough.

'The Minister' is a poem of immense power, of deep bitterness
and (ironically despite its length) as terse and abrupt in its phrasing
as anything the poet has written. It is saved from the irretrievable
negation the poet knowingly risks, by the piercing power of his perceptions, and by the way that the poet's metaphoric sense of the
physical world is identified with the main sustaining metaphor
behind the poem's story.This is the empty moor, endless, dark and
inscrutable, which we feel perhaps would be God himself or the
place where God might have been. That suggests a comparison with
the end of David Jones' *The Sleeping Lord*; but in 'The Minister' the
echoes of T.S. Eliot are strongest and also even of an *Under Milk
Wood* gone sour. The presence of Milton hovers here too, in the
strong biblical anger; and when, after a local political meeting the
villagers walk home "arguing confusedly under the stars", one half-
hears Satan's followers "in wand'ring mazes lost" as they try
hopelessly to discuss theological points from their unlikely position.
Certainly the theme of 'The Minister', if not diabolical, is that of a
community a long way from the neighbourly love which is presumably a pre-requisite if one would regain paradise.

The poem moves between the two clear markers of the destroyed
gospel of Christianity at the outset:

> "Beloved, let us love one another," the words are blown
> To pieces by the unchristened wind

> In the chapel rafters, and love's text
> Is riddled by the inhuman cry
> Of buzzards circling above the moor

and the poem's very last, damning words:

> Wrong from the start, for nature's truth
> Is primary and her changing seasons
> Correct out of a vaster reason
> The vague errors of the flesh.

"Wrong from the start"; and since the lines of narration in the story are very lucid and strongly sequential, all its events are ruthlessly sent to perdition by this one short phrase, as though all was so evil, so desperate, that it would have been better for none of it to have ever happened, nor even the tradition behind it ("Protestantism - the adroit castrator/Of art; the bitter negation/Of song and dance .and the heart's innocent joy"), which gave rise to the chapel in the bare hills where the story is set.

The poet's astonishing metaphoric resources are proliferated at many levels, from the searing ironic play on single words, to extended passages of great, and in context equally ironic, beauty. The poet is rather more than either the narrator or the minister, both of whom speak in their own voices. However the narrator also broadly gives the poet's own message and evident emotions, and this lets him make the central inferences himself and also stand back from the sharp, unlovely interplay between the minister Morgan and the manipulative and lascivious chapel deacon Job Davies. Davies controls the chapel's life and affairs, and reduces the minister to an impotence through which, however, he learns the unpalatable truths of (as Davies puts it) "how things is managed in the hills here".

In characteristic fashion Thomas begins with a romanticism which then gets a dose of cold reality:

> This is the land of green hay
> And greener corn, because of the long
> Tarrying of winter and the late spring.
> This is the land where they burn peat
> If there is time for cutting it,
> And the weather improves for drying it,
> And the cart is not too old for carrying it
> And doesn't get stuck in the wet bog.

The upstaging of what has been said by an abrupt last-word comment is found in many passages in the poem. It is mainly
responsible, along with the ironic double-meanings of single words,
for the poem's ruthlessly realistic effect. Later, the effect is the same,
when Morgan has had early successes with his particular mode of
hwyl-exploiting evangelistic preaching at chapel services (again this
is the end of a passage):

> The whole chapel was soon ablaze.
> Except for the elders, and even they were moved
> By the holy tumult, but not extremely.
> They knew better than that.

Consequently, the early passage in which Thomas cites the powerful Welsh revivalists of the Methodist tradition is partly ironical,
although the actual celebration of their mystical communion with
the divine through the natural is genuinely believed. This however
makes the passage wistful, and so the more poignant:

> O, but God is in the throat of a bird;
> Ann heard Him speak, and Pantycelyn.
> God is in the sound of the white water
> Falling at Cynfal. God is in the flowers
> Sprung at the feet of Olwen, and Melangell
> Felt His heart beating in the wild hare.
> Wales in fact is His peculiar home,
> Our fathers knew Him. But where is that voice now?

Thomas here touches on an idea which has had some place in the
Welsh tradition of preaching and of nationalism; that of the chosen
people. The parallels with Moses and the Israelites enslaved by the
Egyptians but determined by history, and God, to move to freedom
by spreading God's word, were not uncommonly cited during the
high moments of Welsh nonconformity. The passage suggests not
mere irony here. Thomas may not have believed it, though some
poems later suggest he may have yearned for it on occasion. His
own laser-beam perception of what is the case, however, one which
spreads through his later work as he reads the irreversible impact of
the whole of modern technology on both Wales and England, means
he introduces the idea only as a fleeting glimpse. When it comes to
choosing a minister here and now, the reality is different:

                              Let him learn
His calling first, and choose after
Among our girls, if he must marry.
There's your girl, Pugh; or yours, Parry;
Ministers' wives they ought to be
With those white hands that are too soft
For lugging muck or pulling a cow's
Tits. But ay, he must be young.
Remember that mare of yours, John?

The speaker is the deacon Job Davies. His coarse language, his revolting chauvinism toward women, his instinctive thought of them and the minister as part of his own farmyard stock, his erection of money as all and his mean bullying of the young appointee, seem an expression of the whole gamut of traditional Protestant small-community vices, the very ones the New Testament is most continually at pains to expunge. Davies seduces a girl, Buddug, young enough to be his daughter (perhaps granddaughter), and bribes the minister with bits of extra food. But then when Morgan accuses him of adultery he turns on the nasty side:

Take a word from me and keep your nose
In the Black Book, so it won't be tempted
To go sniffing where it's not wanted.
And leave us farmers to look to our own
Business, in case the milk goes sour
From your sharp talk before it's churned
To good butter, if you see what I mean.

"Buddug" plays on dug, and R.S. Thomas's peremptory dismissal of any clerical squeamishness of language gives free rein to a scatological vocabulary of tits, bugger, dung, pus, muck, "the moon's bum" and the rest – routine today, but strong stuff for a rural vicar in the nineteen fifties. But this continues a wider vocabulary in Thomas, especially strong near the start of *Song at the Year's Turning*, and one that has a libidinous relish for immersion in the liquid, glutinous and messy. Bilge, sweat and muck abound. In its own turn this reaches out to a wider circle still of verbs, like "sniffing" and "churned" here, where a small physical agitation is present. It is essential to the texture of the verse, the wider effect of immersing the landscape's inhabitants into a limiting, near-sighted engagement with what is only seen as broad beautiful landscape, by

people of a certain level of refinement and education. Again this
raises the matter of how far those without those things are responsible for their own limitations.

If Morgan had been a saint, he might have resisted Davies's ulti-
mately debilitating sensuality, and even his short-term wiliness. But
there are no saints in the Dissenting church, only religious revolu-
tionaries and charismatic heroes. An underlying theme of 'The
Minister' is that the way to broaden one's mind and spirit, to oneself as well as to the community and wider world, must be through
openness to nature. But this is not an unconsidered romanticism.
Thomas's point (despite his own averred dislike of cities and towns)
is that this is necessary for the chapel minister and farmers, because
the undeveloped natural world is where they happen to live. Morgan
"never listened to the hills'/Music" or even knew the names of the
birds. Instead, he pulled up some flowers planted round the manse
by an earlier occupant, and sprinkled cinders there instead. Our own
sophisticated technological outlook may see much of Davies's
behaviour as at least comprehensible and not so very shocking; and
we may also find our orientation to nature as set-scene landscapes
without humans, as something we have left behind. Our natural
world now, like Thomas's in later books such as *Frequencies*, has a
galactic dimension and is impregnated by relatively futuristic components and forces; the sub-atomic particle, quasars, the gene, and
nuclear power. But in the context of 'The Minister' the effect is convincing. This is because, although Job Davies outwits the minister,
the poet himself is a further step ahead still in the fulness of his
apprehension. It is he who presents and creates Davies and Morgan
in the first place, but then sets them in a context which only the poet
has the spiritual antennae to intuit:

> The bare moor, where nature brooded
> Over her old, inscrutable secret.

In the end, in part at least, Morgan too finds this solution.
"Morgan was learning/To hold his tongue, the wisdom of the moor".
This takes us to a different kind of poem.

Morgan was reduced to silence. Was he balked by silence? That
question is asked in the poem 'In a Country Church' which occurs
nearly at the end of *Song at the Year's Turning*. The poem is the first
of many to be written during the years in which a man prays alone

in an empty church. The atmosphere could hardly be more different from that of 'The Minister'. Thomas's role as lonely priest is another topic, gradually separating again from that of the peasant or of his nation.

The empty church as prayer's context does not appear explicitly again in these first three books, and its later increasing frequency may have resulted from a decline in church attendances and support in rural parishes over the years. There was also the increasing loneliness Thomas records in the somewhat hostile parish of Eglwysfach in the later part of this period. Nevertheless there are two other poems, 'Bread' in *Poetry for Supper* and 'Judgement Day' in *Tares*, which also express a solitary man's engagement with God. These three poems are each a spiritual intensification, as though the moment of prayer and its silence have to be matched, in words' contrasting articulation, by strong concentrations of static metaphor that could not come in the world of discursive speech.

I feel that 'In a Country Church' is the nodal spiritual poem in the first two books, just as 'Welsh Landscape' is the nodal lyric poem of Wales. The first line, "To one kneeling down no word came", already suggests something remarkable. A poet-priest of all people, someone who has access to two verbal traditions of great historical and cultural power, is reduced to silence in the setting of the church building itself, and in presumed confrontation with that church's god. In the early poems, culminating in 'A Priest to His People' and its waves of rhetorical question, the priest was not at all silent. 'Out of the Hills', ' A Labourer', 'Song', 'Ire', 'Memories', 'Chapel Deacon', 'Valediction', 'Priest and Peasant' and other poems all consist of questions asked, but very easily, as though the poet is not at a loss to articulate them, and even finds relish in expressing them. This strain quietens later as the priest finds that neither his flock, nature or God will answer. The first line faces the change, but there is a replacement:

> To one kneeling down no word came,
> Only the wind's song, saddening the lips
> Of the grave saints, rigid in glass;
> Or the dry whisper of unseen wings,
> Bats not angels, in the high roof.
>
> Was he balked by silence? He kneeled long,
> And saw love in a dark crown

Of thorns blazing, and a winter tree
Golden with fruit of a man's body

Unforgettably, the poem is first aural, then visual. Instead of a word there is "only the wind's song", two long notes of elusive hollow music which is "saddening the lips/Of the grave saints, rigid in glass", as though they and their beliefs once lived, but are now congealed in an antiquated art form. There is then the rustle of the "dry whisper of unseen wings,/ Bats not angels" in the roof. This rich fertile imagery means the poet is not balked by silence even though he stays silent. Instead he sees, and prayer's attitude reveals "love in a dark crown/ Of thorns blazing". The physical vigour of the participle seems to contrast with the mud, slime and rain of what has preceded in other poems. Not now staring, the poet now seems visionary. Such detail as "lips" and "golden with fruit" show that the poet's capacity for spiritual reception and physical eyesight can yield metaphors that feel superhuman and sensuous at once. As a result of his waiting on God, a grace from outside can enter the human space made available. That at least is how I take it an orthodox view of grace, and a traditional view of metaphor immediately palpable, would combine to describe what is said. As in 'The Minister', what survives in an otherwise hopeless position is an extraordinary figurative power, perhaps just because other ways are closed. It must have left Thomas in huge dilemmas, if his calling demanded a more social, active response to the conditions his parishioners had to wrestle with for their lifetimes.

The poem 'Bread' acknowledges this social dimension. The God is not present, only the desperate praying, brought on, it seems, by some acid piece of gossip the poet may have unwittingly overheard, sublimated as "the pitiless candour of the stars'/Talk". He therefore prays immediately "in an old byre", which he happens to be near. The need is not for food or warmth but for love. Again that is, the power to love takes the form of an answering grace, in an image which the reader cannot avoid seeing before his or her own eyes: "the white loaf on the white snow". On receiving the power of love he prayed for, the priest rose and "broke/Like sun crumbling the gold air/The live bread for the starved folk". We seem to see dust in a shaft of sunlight.

The last line, "the live bread for the starved folk", is portentous in a way a secular world probably finds hard to take. Such confidence in the priestly role cannot be so easily sustained now. But there is no doubting the pressure of the experience on the priest on this occasion. The last line sounds rather wistful, as though that strong monosyllabic formulation could bring a traditional possibility back into being, and make it true. The poem's pulse is not the calm, if sad, one of 'In a Country Church', where the poet waits within silence. There is some agitation in the negatives and repetitive urgencies: "not for food...not for warmth...He prayed for love, love that would share...". This agitation makes for some intellectual insistence too, which the stable sacramentality of the final lines of the other poem did not need: "to pray was to know...warmth brought the rain's/ Blurring of the essential point...". Yet it is the metaphoric presence that we most remember, and the question will be how far that is the poet's true interest, his real and – until at the earliest *Laboratories of the Spirit* – his only route to confrontation with God.

God is seldom mentioned in these first books. In 'Judgement Day' God ("Lord") is addressed directly, and the poet is, or ends (it is ambiguous), kneeling. But the poem begins with the poet seeing only himself. He seems to be looking in a mirror and, as so often with Thomas, the start is an incident in passing: "Yes, that's how I was/I know that face...". On the other hand, bearing in mind the poem's title, it might be a conceit about arrival into God's presence after death, at which point a mirror is silently held up to confront each newcomer. What matters is that the poet's thoughts are now metaphysical in cast. There is not the obdurate, tangible presence of objects one by one of the other two poems; the stained-glass windows, the singing wind, the white loaf on the snow. Here rather the looking-glass is felt by the reader suddenly, as a small surprise, halfway through. It has to be earned:

> Lord, breathe once more
> On that sad mirror,
> Let me be lost
> In mist forever
> Rather than own
> Such bleak reflections.
> Let me go back
> On my two knees...

It is John Donne, not John Milton or John Keats who this time breathes a self-knowingly penitent life into this passage. Instead of the robust entities of sun, fire, apple and bread we have the sort of double-meaning conceit which Thomas will use again and again in future poems. "Reflections" is so obvious a pun that considerable tact is needed in its use. Thomas succeeds, for another double meaning has anticipated it in 'own'. The poem is confessional, not in the way of Lowell or Plath, but of Augustine in its more originary sense. To lay one's soul bare to God is both to own it and to own up to it. And the misting over of the mirror seems deliberately to eliminate any strong image which, in this kind of poem, would distract. The mirror too will recur many times in future poems. The progress of this line of approach from 'In a Country Church' to 'Judgement Day' is thin in mere number of poems; but it reveals the poet becoming aware of what eventually will have to be his kind of discourse, if the spiritually prototypical and traditional figure of the lone man with God is to be presented acceptably to a modern reader. That is also if, in short, Thomas himself is to practise a religious life with some affinities to the mystic rather than the pastor.

These then are the main themes of these first three books: the peasant, Wales, the pastoral priest inveighing, and briefly the holy man praying and watching. These figures are rooted in a landscape, and the third book's title goes on underlining that theme. A tare is inimical to corn crops but is a root nonetheless. It implies faults, but very human ones. However, in *Tares* and in the first two books there are interlaced a number of other poems on rather more wide-ranging subjects. They fill in the picture and show Thomas latently preparing for a considerably fuller expansion in the books to come. It might be worth briefly examining a few of these poems and their themes, before concluding this chapter by discussing what, as has been suggested, seems to be Thomas's real source and central need as a poet. That is to say, his expression of metaphoric power. Many of these poems, naturally, evince such power, and indeed the departure from his own dominating themes and the opportunity to tap imagery from their wider locations makes for greater power.

The most obvious of these other preoccupations are literature, music and painting; and Thomas's own wife and family. All of these get far greater elaboration in the books ahead. Among the most compelling are two in *Tares* which are about musicians, 'The Conductor' and 'The Musician'. In both of these the inseparable union of musician and music is suggested but with opposing spiritual implication. Both, that is, are analogues of a spiritual condition, although 'The Conductor' is an extended metaphor while 'The Musician' describes a real event at a concert. 'The Conductor' starts with an extraordinary physical evocation, made metaphor by the one word "stars":

> Finally at the end of the day
> When the sun was buried and
> There was no more to say,
>
> He would lift idly his hand,
> And softly the small stars'
> Orchestra would begin

The end however suggests spiritual pride. Making sure no disharmony "troubled the deep peace",

> It was this way he adored
> With a god's ignorance of sin
> The self he had composed.

If 'he' is other than God then self-centredness would appear to be the passage's force. But even if God is referred to, it raises old theological questions as to how God can be both omnipotent and all-loving. The import is very different from that expressed in later books, where God's side, rather than that of Adam or Jesus, bears the wounds, and where all kinds of people, not Jesus alone, are nailed to a tree.

In 'The Musician' the import is the opposite one from spiritual pride. A concert audience is enthralled at the musician Kreisler's virtuoso performance, "because it was himself that he played". But this time the performer sacrifices himself rather than imposes himself. As in all the peasant poems the poet closely watches. The unusual circumstances of this give the poem its convincingly realistic touch, enabling the broader religious symbol to emerge very naturally:

> The seats all taken, I found myself pushed
> On to the stage with a few others,
> So near that I could see the toil
> Of his face muscles, a pulse like a moth
> Fluttering under the fine skin,
> And the indelible veins of his smooth brow.

I could see, too, the twitching of the fingers,
Caught temporarily in art's neurosis,
As we sat there or warmly applauded
This player who so beautifully suffered
For each of us upon his instrument.

So it must have been on Calvary...

The crucified man hangs on the cross much as the player is
entwined with his large instrument. It is worth noting parenthetically
Thomas's verbal accuracy in the word "indelible", the old pencils
used by grocers and butchers before supermarket days having
exactly the blue tinge of veins. The two poems are fine examples of
how Thomas can introduce a wholly different cultural dimension
into the spiritual explorations incurred in his engagement with his
farm people, and in his own spiritual yearnings which emerge in 'In
a Country Church' and 'Judgement Day'. Both the music poems
have very clear outlines and profiles; they feel contained wholly in
themselves, and so they show the poet's usual preoccupations in different context.

Something similar is true of 'A Person from Porlock'. Here
Thomas himself is interrupted by a visitor when writing a poem, as
Coleridge claimed to have been when he was writing *Kubla Khan*.
Thomas, too, finds he cannot finish it when left alone again. But the
point is, that the poet's study with table and books sets a delineated
scene comparable to that of the concert hall. It is a way of indicat-
ing to the reader already attuned to Thomas's usual rural setting,
that some quite different import is to emerge, in this case a certain
introversion found also in 'Phobia'.

In writing of his own family, Thomas touches on matters which
come into the open much more in later books. The clearest example is 'Anniversary', which it seems was written when Thomas had
been married nineteen years. The spareness of tone turns out not to
distract from the silent marital unity that underlies it. The poem has
the poet and his wife at a meal; the sharing of food is implicitly
sacramental, but in a secular mode, as though intelligence is the diet
most needful; and marriage's potential for bliss or pain has to be
controlled:

Nineteen years now
Sharing life's table,

And not to be first
To call the meal long
We balance it thoughtfully
On the tip of the tongue,
Careful to maintain
The strict palate.

"On the tip of the tongue"; that is to say at the point of speech. The poet is carefully letting his readers see, in part, what supports his two chosen vocations: there is no false sentiment, no fulsome gratitude, only a single fruition all the more positive:

Opening the womb
Softly to let enter
The one child
With his huge hunger.

The Thomases had one child, a son, and he is included though with no detail peculiar to himself in 'Ap Huw's Testament' and (one would imagine, although the mode is more fictional) in 'Mother And Son'. These poems on Thomas's family have a gauged intimacy which is of considerable significance in preparing the reader for the later overtly sexual poems, on which for some reason critics of all persuasions have remained largely silent. 'Walter Llywarch', 'Age' and 'Farm Wife' all begin to stir with this theme in these early books, as does 'Once', where a later much repeated Thomas compulsion first emerges:

in his eye
The light of the cracked lake

That once she had propped to comb
Her hair in.

As the later books unfold, the matters of sex and of Thomas himself as family man, particularly in relation to his own father, are elaborated in more detail, and we are able to understand the poet more deeply. This first period only touches on these things. However, the intimacy which is enabled by the closeness of family table, house and study gives Thomas an opportunity to write about certain other individuals, not now the peasants themselves, seen closely and therefore uniquely. Their condition seems to arise from,

or most imaginatively result in, their unique selves. With the peasants, the social and physical conditions so dominate, that it is not
often that a single farmer emerges recognizably in that way. This is
no fault in the poetry, for the prototype burdened by nature and
exploitation is what Thomas apparently wanted to put across. But
in 'Phobia' for instance, we see a very different aspect of human
suffering:

> This poor woman who was afraid,
> Afraid of the gestures the trees made
> In the wood at night or on the blind
> The intestinal rumour, the ripe swell
> Of muscles under the taut skin;
> Through long brooding conceived at last
> Peculiar sickness, nurtured it
> And reared it, till it was of age
> To practice incest with its mother.
> From such foul intercourse death came
> Bloodily forth.
>   Take her cold hand,
> Spirit, and lead her gently away
> From the mind's darkness into the light,
> If not the comfort, of truth's flame.

The double meanings are not just puns, for "brooding" and
"conceived" have significances both sexual and intellectual which
are clearly deeply connected, and which Thomas exploits with great
economy. The frightening insight also has some universal import,
cognitive and Sophoclean perhaps, and the conclusion is a sad
catharsis, evoking some good power to take the woman away into a
"light" which seems in part the lamp that leans over in a doctor's
surgery or psychoanalyst's consulting-room. Doubtless the poem
comes from true experience, but is certainly not confined to rural
communities or to Wales; and if 'social conditions' in any way pre-
disposed this event, that is not where the poem's emphasis lies. The
psychological insight is inseparably embodied in the metaphor of
introversion.

In 'The Evacuee' there is certainly a much happier, sunlit atmosphere, but again it is unique. The picture is somewhat idealised, and
the country people receiving the uprooted girl in war-time are rendered "patient and strong". But the setting is so immediate, in the
farmhouse at dawn:

> She woke up under a loose quilt
> Of leaf patterns, woven by the light
> At the small window, busy with the boughs
> Of a young cherry..,
>   she would have crept
> Uneasily from the bedroom with its frieze
> Of fresh sunlight, had not a cock crowed,
> Shattering the surface of that limpid pool
> Of stillness, and before the ripples died
> One by one in the field's shallows,
> The farm woke with uninhibited din.

It is as though the girl's unexpected presence let the poet, as well as the farmers (the "farm faces trying to be kind"), take their minds temporarily off their endless burdens and, in the poet's case, revel in certain physical manifestations for which he has so much affection.

Again, in some poems there is a personal longing. Once or twice the poet is at his study window looking out, as in 'The View from the Window' and 'A Blackbird Singing'. In both of these the poet is moved to tears. This response is like the wistfulness which emerges more generally in the next period, which begins with *The Bread of Truth* and in which standing at the study window is the occasion sometimes of feelings of failure or even self-disgust. This, one suspects, is the period when the church generally is gradually losing its hold on the community, and the rural clergyman, poet or not, cannot but re-examine his role with the fullest honesty, however painful it is. The well-known poem 'The Country Clergy' touches on the matter, and there is a touch of the same longing in 'The Letter', where the poet appears to have heard from abroad and, rarely for him, seen urban civilization in an ideal light:

> And to be able to put at the end
> Of the letter Athens, Florence – some name
> That the spirit recalls from earlier journeys
>   ...cities and towns
> Where the soul added depth to its stature.
>
> And not to worry about the date,
> The words being timeless, concerned with truth...

The sense of flight away, not surprisingly, is an undertone when Thomas writes of birds, as in the poem on the blackbird just cited,

and also 'Winter Starlings', with its very strong echo of Wallace
Stevens in thought and movement. Only rarely here does a poem
express happiness. One feels in reading all these poems a considerable sympathy for Thomas, though he did not seek it. On the
contrary, I suggest there is a strong repression at work. Thomas's
inner poetic drive had to be harnessed to the cause of the peasants
and of Wales, and one senses that he was here seeking a way of
using his considerable literacy and classical learning, and his more
mystical intuitions, and had not yet found it. Just once in these early
books Thomas finds a case where the scene immediately before him
can be matched with a cosmic perspective to make not a stressful
tension but a calm equilibrium:

> So little happens; the black dog
> Cracking his fleas in the hot sun
> Is history. Yet the girl who crosses
> From door to door moves to a scale
> Beyond the bland day's two dimensions.
>
> Stay then, village, for round you spins
> On slow axis a world as vast
> And meaningful as any poised
> By great Plato's solitary mind.
>   ('The Village')

Finally there are a number of poems in which Thomas presents
nature as symbol. Here the theme is neither that of nature-lover nor
rural inhabitant struggling to make a living, and in fact the world is
only secondarily inhabited by human beings. Rather, nature
emanates from a different order of things. Sometimes the symbol-
ism of traditional Christian theology is made new:

> Who said to the trout,
> You shall die on Good Friday
> To be food for a man
> And his pretty lady?
>
> It was I, said God,
> Who formed the roses
> In the delicate flesh
> And the tooth that bruises.
>   ('Pisces')

The sharp intrusion of the formal "pretty lady" into the world red in tooth and claw, and the trout as spoken to, take the poet away from any secular inference. In 'Siesta', an apparently ordinary visit to the sea shore takes Thomas away from his usual bleak pastoral concerns, with a resulting picture vastly expanded and in the end surreal:

> ...watching the sky's blue
> Room awhile through the air's window,
> They saw it furnished with tall cloud,
> And habitable by some huge presence
> At whose stature the mind balked.

If 'Pisces' is a mediaeval Passion carol, this is a Magritte painting, with a wardrobe in the sky. In 'Alpine' Thomas gets clear of the everyday scene by a prosaic hill climb, but again poetic perception is correspondingly lifted by the end. The opening is straightforward; "About mountains it is useless to argue,/You have either been up or you haven't"; but the end is a different kind of insight:

> walking on clouds
> Through holes in which you can see the earth
>
> Like a rich man through the eye of a needle.
> The mind has its own level to find.

In these poems along with 'Winter', 'The Cat and the Sea', and some others, Thomas is able to suggest a way of seeing nature available to humans only if they can temporarily put aside their actual circumstances, and if by intelligence or good fortune long internalized they have the means, available from a cultural inheritance, to do so. Like all these more miscellaneous and wider reaching poems we have considered, they point up more sharply, and both severely and compassionately at once, the narrowed vision of people who must grapple with mere survival only. The discipline and vocation entailed in those other poems, characteristically centring on the peasant, are underlined.

In this last group of poems R.S. Thomas's very strong metaphorical power expands itself to a point at which the whole poem is an allegory of some larger entity, or is a physical symbol of a spiritual condition. This is very clear with 'Alpine'. But in these early books for the most part he did not try this. As a result, as we have seen, metaphorical expressions of great intensity and vivid force have usually seemed to burst out from the poem's everyday story and then subside again. Thus, raising a distinction between metaphor and symbol, one can say that the early Thomas is, on the face of it at least, normally metaphorical. We shall have to return to this distinction later, but for the present this is a good point at which to consider the matter of Thomas's metaphors more specifically. Many readers have remarked on them, and have come to value them greatly. Are they simply a poetic gift, or are they something to do with Thomas's priestly vocation as well? What can we say about them?

Thomas's early poetry proliferates with sets of clear evocations of fundamental and palpable entities: tree, rain, hill, sky, soil, river, fire, cup, animal, peasant, stone, flower, field, family, bread. They may gradually accrue into symbolic reference or general pattern, but what we primarily remember is their immediate startling impact. The undernourished labourer's ribs are "bare racks of bone", the earth "feels the plough/Probing her womb", a man's ribs elsewhere are a "trellised thicket, where the heart, that robin,/Greets with a song the seasons of the blood". In derelict farmhouses "the grass.../Grew from the chimney-stack like smoke." More generally, one notes that the list given at the start of this paragraph is consistent with a certain setting and way of life. The metaphoric terms any poet uses will depend on his or her particular and personal response to where they were found; the people, jobs, technology, and landscape and trees and animals the poet is near. Indeed, although the response varies from poet to poet the ingredients available will depend strongly on the environment. Thomas lived close to the natural world. One of his commonest bases for metaphor is rain. The country road is "fenced with rain", the farmer's coat is "seamed with rain" or it is "a sack, pinned at the corners/With the rain's drops", and the minister wakes to see the rain "Spitting and clawing at the pane". In all these cases it is not the rain that is metaphor of something else; it is that the rain commonly is the occasion on which something else is drawn in as a comparison. An equally common basis is cloud. Prytherch "pens a few sheep in a gap of cloud", habit "drapes" the labourer "on a bush of cloud", and in one beautiful Wordsworthian pairing of inner and outer

> the tall clouds sail
> Westward full-rigged, and darken with their shadow
> The bright surface as a thought the mind
> ('Enigma')

Yet what one notices in this last example is that, although the comparison with reflective thought is present, the strong metaphor is between clouds and sailing ships. That is to say, both terms of the metaphor are physical. The pairing and comparing of two physical things in R.S. Thomas is exceedingly common. Outside the dying Evans's house is "the one tree/Weather-tortured". Prytherch's "sharp eyes" are "bright as thorns". The landscape is a painting where "all through history/ The great brush has not rested,/Nor the paint dried". The farm boy has a smooth face like "a finch's egg".

All these metaphors are, as literary theorists were once fond of putting it, 'literally untrue', and this mode of sharp-edged 'untrue' comparison shares a susceptibility peculiar to poets where a strong mythic base is at work with great constraining force, in this case Protestantism. In Protestantism, perhaps paradoxically, there is a sacramental freedom to combine and recombine a set of entities found in a starkly unelaborated world. In the Catholic tradition the places of blood, bread, table, light and the rest are already incorporated into a complex theological structure which is also already symbolic, so that the metaphorical power of the terms is pre-empted. The Protestant tradition on the other hand, suspicious of both idolatry and luxury, can only counter a threatening dogmatic literalism by the power of its metaphors to be literally and compellingly untrue. The more literal and non-symbolic the mythic source, the more robust and vigorous are the resulting metaphors generated from that base. They are, as the American critic Ted Cohen once put it, "fully-fledged metaphors". There is no ambiguity about them, no double meaning in individual words or word-play is yet associated with them, and it is notable that Thomas moves out to this sort of word-play only gradually in his poetic career. Of course, one cannot mechanically predict that a Catholic poet will use fewer sharp metaphors than a Protestant one, for too much else is involved in terms of degree of orthodoxy, type of individual's apprehension of the world, and so on. But it is not surprising that a poet of strong Protestant background who lives close to nature by choice and so in a 'simplified' rather than pluralized world, should write in this way, if he has the gift and the notion of 'gift' has any valency. Thomas's metaphors impress themselves on the reader's mind directly.

But how then can the metaphor be both 'literally untrue' and yet also powerful? We can speak of this in both secular and religious terms; according to literary theory and according to theology. Considerable advances in the twentieth century in our understanding of how language works have affected metaphor itself. It was once common to see metaphor as merely a comparison between two things, speaking of one in terms of the other. But since Wittgenstein and earlier, language itself has less often seemed to refer reliably to reality, name for thing. Rather it is the way we attempt to convey our idea of reality to each other, to get across to each other. If this is true, then metaphor fills space in order to gain various kinds of attention. Almost all language is metaphorical, for if no language reliably refers to reality, no language is literal. We must then say that obvious or 'fully-fledged' metaphors are striking examples, new and local cases. Further back and wider than that is a pattern of characteristic figures by which a whole way of life is customarily expressed. Further back still are the deepest shapes and forms of language itself.

In this early period R.S. Thomas deployed the immediate metaphor with such impact and success that it became his poetry's central characteristic. He could do so just because he had a relatively certain set of beliefs about the physical world he inhabits. His metaphors, typically of this kind, do not tell the (literal) truth, they put matter to work. It is not words but things that are sharply compared. Such metaphorical statements can only be powerful while not literally the case, if the objects compared remain clearly distinct from each other, and do not blur into each other. In a sloppy metaphor or cliché this may not be so. Thus the moving clouds and full-rigged ships, and the human heart in the rib-cage and the robin in the trellis, remain vivid and separate in the reader's picture. But equally, it has to be clear which term in the comparison is the solid object before the poet's eye, and which is the one drawn in as metaphorical extension. Clearly Thomas is seeing clouds and a man, and imagining full-rigged ships and a robin. If this principle of distinction were not observed our attention could be distractingly divided. The critic I.A. Richards distinguished between the 'tenor' and the 'vehicle' in a metaphor in order to underline this distinction; the theorist Max Black called them the 'principal' and the 'subsidiary'. In the cases cited from Thomas it is clear where his principal attention lies. As well as the two just referred to, we may also say that, in the examples given a few paragraphs back, he is attending to the tree, the landscape and the farm boy, not the torture, the painting or the egg. Of course he must be interested in those things too, otherwise he would not be drawn by them into generating new meaning, new ways of seeing common features in a disparate world. But at the moment of writing it is clear what his subject is. The subsidiary terms, however, become luminous in the mind's eye. They enrich the subject, which stays quietly beside this new glowing feature given to it.

Thomas never ceases to go on generating these extraordinary comparisons. But as he does so, some metaphors appear more than others. This is the case for both halves of the figure. His 'principals', at first anyway, are drawn from the local world he inhabits; the labourers, church, fields, trees and sky. The close relation of these to each other in the real world ensures that the world written about is consistent and recognizable no matter what metaphors are proliferated. We illustrated this by showing how often rain and cloud were tenor and principal. But some of the subsidiary terms too, the comparisons themselves, also recur more and more frequently. With Thomas the commonest are the bone, tree and mirror, although there are others. In these cases, especially with the mirror, they recur as the means of the metaphor, not the thing for which a metaphor is sought. The lake as mirror, the field as mirror, the woman's eye as mirror, all occur. Unsurprisingly, Thomas does not draw on the urban world for comparisons, certainly not at this stage, for he is not thinking of that world. Yet his fertility of invention is astonishing, and for that reason his new metaphors remain prominent, even in later periods when he becomes dissatisfied with a world-view that attaches such substantive reality to language. But these other more common metaphors just cited last longer, and they take on a richness of meaning as they are increasingly employed. The bone is the human centre both continuous and real, and stripped-down and exposed. The tree becomes living knowledge which is sacrificial; the mirror is self-knowledge which is painful. That is to say, these metaphors gradually turn into symbols, and this is the distinction we made earlier. Indeed to encapsulate them into a phrase as I have done, though possibly helpful in the short run, is to reduce them.

The same matter of metaphor, Protestantism and literal untruth can be put into religious and theological terms. The American theologian

Sally McFague cites the occasion when Martin Luther whispered under his breath the words "and is not" after being forced to repeat out loud the liturgical statement "this [bread] is the body of Christ". (Luther's aim was to retain his integrity over transubstantiation. The question of whether bread and wine do really or only symbolically turn into Christ's flesh and blood at Mass or communion, has been of course a centuries-old topic of contention between the Protestant and Catholic faiths.) McFague argues that this incident in Luther's life illustrates well the Protestant tradition's use of metaphor. The Protestant protests, says defiantly that some tenet or belief is not so. But Luther allowed the "is" too; he only said "and is not". He added the "is not", he did not substitute it. If the poetic metaphors contained literal untruth and nothing more, there would be no point in them. Therefore, in Thomas's metaphors, the cloud both is and is not a full-rigged ship, and a peasant's mind both is and is not cold ash in the hearth when a fire has gone out. The prototype metaphor in Protestantism is Jesus Christ himself, who both is and is not God, is both man and God.

And, as McFague also points out, this "is-not" quality has shock-value. This shock-value is characteristic of the parables in the Gospels, in which a loyal eldest son gets only the same inheritance as his brother who is a waster, and workers in a vineyard for one hour get paid as much as those who worked all day. It is the central, energizing thrust of Protestant poetry over the centuries, found in Herbert, Milton, Wordsworth, Browning and many more. Understandably then, from this viewpoint, it is Protestantism that has valued the written scriptures and Catholicism the handed-down sacramental rites.

In poetry furthermore this shock-value can be seen as the reason why metaphors are seldom merely a delightful surprise. They are also often shocking, in our usual sense of the word which makes us say that something ought not to be as it is. Thomas himself used the word when talking of his early experience as a rural priest:

> Well, I came out of a kind of bourgeois environment which, especially in modern times, is protected; it's cushioned from some of the harsher realities; and this muck and blood and hardness, the rain and the spittle and the phlegm of farm life was, of course, a shock to begin with and one felt that this was something not quite part of the order of things.

In "muck", "blood", "phlegm", "spittle" and of course "rain" we see many of the objective realities Thomas incorporated into his powerful and telling metaphorical pictures. And we realise that here we have, in poetry, one of those profound and disturbing connections that poetry makes, and which have troubled philosophers and ordinary people from time immemorial; namely, the meeting-point of the beautiful and the moral. In plainer terms, what ought to make us ashamed or disgusted also gives pleasure. I suspect the secret is that this too "is and is not"; that a thing ought not to be so, and is giving thousands pain and suffering, but because it still is so nonetheless, it is real, part of the real world, and should at least be made as dignified and indeed as lovely as possible. The temptation for the comfortable reader is to enjoy the pleasure and quietly suppress the squalidness and dirt. The irony then is that we are left in the same beauty-morality dilemma as before.

More widely, it seems that this is what Thomas understands by the traditional gospel story and its relation to poetry. Jesus ought not to have been murdered by jealous authorities. Yet having gone through that ordeal he survives it (is resurrected), and in just the same way as conventional Christianity cannot leave it that he was an ordinary, if very good, man who happened to have been the victim of violence. Christ's resurrection is traditionally couched in terms of its glory, majesty and so on; in another sense, its beauty. There is a mystery, a meaning of universal significance as to the very nature of reality, and this has to be uncovered. In fact until his latest collections Thomas had nearly nothing to say in his poems about Christ as resurrected, only about him as crucified, and the poet in later years is led on to nothing less than the search for a poetry that will articulate the universal meaning in a wider sense; in some way, in fact, will articulate God. But for the present, even before that time, he is already finding the evocation of the toiling peasantry and the bleak and merely local landscape does not open up his horizons enough. To stay with them is indeed to stay down at their level, have his vision impaired by the same muck and spittle and phlegm. That is the trouble and the dilemma mentioned earlier. Like anyone else, Thomas found the compassion and the contempt hard to separate.

So the poet begins to reach out for other, wider themes. We have already referred to the two poems on musicians and the more psychological probes of 'A Person from Porlock' and 'Phobia'. But those poems still carve out a small piece of life for themselves and

live in a clear framework. The theme of 'Phobia' is incestuous and
that of the Porlock poem is the stillborn. The beauty-morality
dilemma, on the other hand, touches on a wider, more pervading
idea of metaphor, one that is not expressed universally enough by
one-off references to rain, trees and poor people in however remarkable combinations and no matter how cumulative.

Thomas himself spoke of this wider idea of religion as metaphor:

> Christ was a poet, the New Testament is a metaphor, the
> Resurrection is a metaphor... I consider that the Resurrection is
> a metaphorical use of language, as is the Incarnation... My work
> as a poet has to deal with the presentation of imaginative truth.
> [Later in the same passage Thomas calls this imagination "the
> highest means known to the human psyche of getting into con-
> tact with the ultimate reality".] As a priest I am committed to
> the ministry of the word and the ministry of the sacraments.
> Well, word is metaphor, language is sacrament, sacrament is lan-
> guage.

Sacrament as opposed to word is a matter of physical things. In the
orthodox form of our religion it is centred on the physical realities
of bread and wine, flesh and blood. When R.S. Thomas makes flap-
ping curtains or a dripping tree seem unique, he is rendering them
sacramental. That is to say, they become utterly themselves, they
have the power to exclude all else. When a stinking farmer or terri-
fied old woman is rendered in the same way, it is as if they are
turned from mere matter into suffering matter; mere food or soil
become flesh and blood. This is their hurting, metaphorical power.
But Thomas cannot stay with this alone, because the unique is not,
as such, subsumable into categories of cognition and knowledge.
Gradually, as he progresses, the poet begins to see immediately
apprehended cases of things as local occasions of wider reality, and
these can only be known through wider sets of principles. In a
number of the poems in this first period Thomas already avails himself of the epistemological realms by which a more universal
understanding can get some approximation to truth.

There are, for example, the realms of mathematics and science.
We saw the geometric equilibrium in 'The Village', and in the poem
where Thomas finds early the hint of an impasse, 'No Through
Road', he confesses that "Nature's simple equations/In the mind's
precincts do not apply". There, even though it is the last poem in
the first book, he is not yet ready to go on, and "the old lie/Of green

places beckons me still...'". But in 'Temptation of a Poet' in *Poetry for Supper* he asks Prytherch to help him:

> have I not been
> Too long away? There is a flaw
> In your first premise, or else the mind's
> Acid sours the soft light
> That charmed me.

By now two cognitive modes, the logical and the scientific, are explicitly cited. And both these poems are about going on or going back; elsewhere the often used image of "the mind's lenses" suggests an awareness that his seeing, his compulsive staring, must make and perhaps already is making itself aware of the new attitudes to the world that technology offers. I feel the image of lenses is tied to the equally frequent use of the mirror, which Thomas will later come to use as a continuous metaphor of self-consciousness and self-knowledge. We saw it used in 'Judgement Day'. In 'Ire', "the floor unscrubbed/Is no mirror for the preening sun", Cynddylan rides to work on his tractor "breaking the fields'/Mirror of silence", and in 'A Day in Autumn' a bird is "preening/ In the lawn's mirror." The significance of Thomas's compulsive staring at landscapes, people and self has been raised to consciousness and never leaves Thomas's poetry from here on.

In *Song at the Year's Turning*, however, this new imagery is not developed. In *Poetry for Supper* even so, and in the first book's final section too, there is a new anxiety of a different kind. As has often been noted, *Poetry for Supper* contains several poems to do with the writing of poetry itself, and 'Temptation of a Poet' is one of these. No coherent theory of poetry is attempted or sought, nor is there much on poetic technique. It is more a vocational encounter. Many of the first lines of these poems betray the latent misgiving: "The temptation is to go back..." ('Temptation of a Poet'), "It will not always be like this" ('A Day in Autumn'), "And to be able to put at the end..." ('The Letter'), "It seems wrong that out of this bird..." ('A Blackbird Singing'), "Listen now, verse should be..." ('Poetry for Supper'), "But what to do? Doctors in verse...", "Prytherch man, can you forgive...?" ('Absolution') and most marked of all, "He never could decide what to write/About..." ('Composition'). In all of these poems the poet ends side-tracked by a metaphor too compelling to allow him to go out into the existential world. In

'Absolution', possibly the most remarkable of these, the poet gives full vent to his confession of his own unsuccessful sallies out into the new world, so that the "forgiveness" Prytherch grants by the end can be sublimated into an extraordinary identification of the poet as transcendent figure, seeking what lay "too close for the mind's lenses to see", but returning with the ancient stars themselves still as his defining background. In 'Composition' ("He never could decide...") the poet "tried truth" and then "tried love", but the result is a seizing up: "Slowly the blood congealed/Like dark flowers saddening a field." And in 'Poetry for Supper' itself, the title poem, the two old poets' argument is ignored by the talk that ran "Noisily by them, glib with prose".

In *Tares*, at last, the new necessary mode just begins to grow. It is only a beginning. But the poet starts to place his own difficulties in the foreground without rhetoric, for they become fundamentally part of the poem's thought and movement. In 'Abersoch' a picture is presented, but instead of a robust metaphoric climax the poet turns in on himself:

> there was that girl
> Riding her cycle, hair at half-mast,
> And the men smoking...
>
> Why do I remember these few things,
> That were rumours of life, not life itself
> That was being lived fiercely, where the storm raged?
> Was it just that the girl smiled,
> Though not at me, and the men smoking
> Had the look of those who have come safely home?

Instead of images, it is the small intellectual nuances that are developed, subtle details of opposition and change: "Rumours of life, not life itself"..." The girl smiled, though not at me". In 'The Watcher', already discussed, there is the resume of the act of watching itself; and in 'Which?' it is not just an attitude to Prytherch but a summary of attitudes. And in a rather unusual poem, 'Poet's Address to the Businessmen', there is an ironic sighting of a different section of the public:

> Gentlemen all,
> At the last crumbfall,

The set of glasses,
The moist eye,
I rise to speak
Of things irrelevant...

It seems then that, interspersed in *Tares* with Thomas's hitherto usual settings in 'Hireling', 'To the Farmer', 'An Old Man' and others, Thomas writes poems which find a new need weighing on himself. The mind in motion with itself is newly activated. In 'Here', which comes very near to the end of *Tares* and which more than any other single poem seems explicitly to mark the end of this first period, Thomas declares:

I am like a tree,
From my top boughs I can see
The footprints that led up to me.

The sacramental object has become the poet himself. He has brought into the open the matter of self-knowledge.

II. Searching, Wintering, Waiting, Wales

(The Bread of Truth 1963, *Pietà* 1966,
Not That He Brought Flowers 1968)*

The boundary between Thomas's first and second periods is not a clear one. It is nowhere near as clear as that between the end of this second period and the one following, when *H'm* heralds a new start. Nevertheless, these next three books taken together do convey a change from the time in which Thomas's subjects, compulsions and figural power were establishing themselves. In these next three books the poet moves into darker and more tangled regions. He is forced into a more existential attitude. The realities of a technological world do not so much affect the upland Welsh landscape, which if anything becomes all the more neglected in the modern era. Rather, these realities turn inside out once and for all traditions, community life and ordinary modes of living. It is not that illusions collapse, for the vigorous embodiments of nature found in the first books were hardly illusory. Rather Thomas gradually recasts his apprehension of those things. The move from the hill-farmers of Manafon to the better-heeled parish of Eglwysfach was evidently a key factor in this change.

His tone becomes dry and wintry. Thomas's irony in the first period leant forward powerfully into its subject. Now it is laid back. The metaphoric power is no less evident, but the metaphor now is seldom coterminous with the poem. It becomes only one mode of response among others. The pointed double meaning of the single word is notably more frequent. Except in a few poems, there is not the ring of achieved song as there was earlier. The more frequent mode is that of a brief response to a passing reflection or incident. The strongly succulent vocabulary of mud, dripping trees and heavy fields is present still, but it does not constitute the poetry's material; it is more spaced out. Prytherch recedes. And personal hurt and pain belong more to twentieth century humanity generally, not just the toiling peasant. In *Pietà*, when the black negation of *accidie* retreats a little, it is spiritual patience rather than just physical endurance that is counselled.

The matter of the poetry is also subjected to a shift. It does not, in fact, stay so clearly in focus, although one can pick out certain emphases that occupy the poet from time to time. In *The Bread of Truth* in many poems Thomas expresses the contemporary predicament of Wales in a new way, and makes the point explicit in the last poem of that book, 'Looking at Sheep'. The subject of Wales is by no means confined to that book although it is predominant there. In *Pietà*, amid poems of varying matter, one can also discern an attempt to make a new religious response possible. The church itself (the building) is the location for this in three or four poems, few but telling, and in 'Pietà', 'Amen', 'Kierkegaard', 'The Moor' and 'Exchange' the spirit finds various correlatives for its yearnings. That is a small number, but is more than in *The Bread of Truth*. In the third book *Not That He Brought Flowers* there are a number of similar poems, but the book's import has no positive religious stance. Rather there are, first of all, several poems in which a single person is observed in some continuous, burdensome predicament, some state of life. This focus is no longer on the peasant alone however, and the poet finds himself increasingly voicing the observer, the 'I' who is compelled into this relentless seeing of many others one by one. As a result the staring is no longer a powerful means to poetic material, but rather something, perhaps a hurt, of his own.

By the end of *Not That He Brought Flowers* there is a mixture of distressing self-examination, at times an inner sense of torment, and boredom. The predominance of the 'I' and the anguished yet listless casting about, not merely for subjects for poetry but also for positive direction or route to follow in the world, take all Thomas's literary and personal control, and sense of overall arrangement and design, to make the poetic progress hold together. Yet, also at the end of this period, the poet is probing into those two central narratives of Christian theology, the Garden of Eden and the crucifixion. This is explicit for the first time. How he comes to find a disturbing identification with these two accounts emerges from a consideration of these three books' poems.

One has to face Thomas's attitudes about Wales squarely from the outset. The Welsh language scholar R.M. Jones has said that the poet's "snarling and melancholy hatred toward the Welsh...is basically a positive and creative hatred", while a certain Anglo-Welsh writer has put it of Thomas, less charitably, that "human love is missing". The present writer sees no reason to accept the second statement, but it has to be recorded. R.M. Jones's more curiously positive shift about so black an emotion depends on his own wider view; namely, that any writing by a Welsh person in English is either merely a branch of English literature (and therefore, he implies, of no interest as such to Welsh people), or it inevitably expresses a "cultural wound". In the poems in *The Bread of Truth* the bitterness toward the Welsh has not yet come to direct accusation. The main theme is the Welsh language. Poems that express protest against the domination of Wales by an external economy usually take a particular topic, as in 'Afforestation' and 'Rose Cottage'. There are also two poems on renowned Welsh patriots, 'A Lecturer' and 'The Patriot', said to be about the poet D. Gwenallt Jones (Gwenallt) and the playwright and writer Saunders Lewis, respectively. But these, as well, are also about the language. 'Welcome' is very straightforward:

> You can come in.
> You can come a long way;
> We can't stop you.
> You can come up the roads
> Or by railway;
> You can land from the air.
> You can walk this country
> From end to end;
> But you won't be inside;
> You must stop at the bar,
> The old bar of speech.

It is not particularly ironic yet, and mildly challenging without being threatening. In 'Looking at Sheep' Thomas colours the air with stronger terms:

>   ...visitors
> Buying us up. Thousands of mouths
> Arc emptying their waste speech
> About us, and an Elsan culture
> Threatens us.

The language is the centre of attention, the rival language is seen as excrement. This is so even when other elements of political and economic domination are present. In the first poem, indeed, it is as though everything except the language is conceded. Elsewhere there is a clue as to why this emphasis pertains:

> At fifty he was still trying to deceive
> Himself. He went out at night,
> Imagining the dark country
> Between the border and the coast
> Was still Wales; the old language
> Came to him on the wind's lips...
> ('A Country')

It seems that, whether or not the country and the language can be identified, the country no longer exists recognizably for its inhabitants. The suggestion might seem at first simply that, political rule having been forfeited historically, the need is to hold on to the indigenous language as the last, but adequate, means of cultural identity and unity. There are still many people in Wales today who speak as if this were so. But with Thomas, while certainly the language is central, the wound seems to have cut very deep indeed. Furthermore, historical as his own general sensibility often seems, his allusions to the actual history of Wales are relatively rare, brief, and always declining. In the early poems in *Song at the Year's Turning* he refers once or twice to the Glyn Dwr rising and to the death of Llywelyn at the hands of Edward I, "the old treachery at the ford", the effective end of Wales as an autonomous political entity in 1282. But after that there is little historical reference. Rather, Thomas's response is to a cultural death and decay which is contemporary. He sees it all about him and it expresses itself in the importance of money; cheap consumer goods ("trash", "baubles" and the rest) and commuter existence; the shallow cultural exploitations of tourism; and the idolatry of science and casual sex, this last usually paraded by girls wearing cheap cosmetics and rubbishy jewellery. Such cultural manifestations are urban in origin, and England is characteristically urban. Wales is not.

One might say to this – as he did himself – that Thomas was a poet, not a nationalist politician whose job was to be conscious of his country's history, and that his role was not to propose action but to stir a people's imagination. Yet I feel it is more than that. One wonders, at times, whether Thomas's despair derived from a feeling that he arrived generations or even centuries too late, and that this feeling was itself a product of a wistful sense of what might have been in an entirely different British dispensation from earlier times. Even after the three drastic events from the Welsh point of view, that is the final victory over Llywelyn, the crushing of Owen Glyn

Dwr's rising in about 1415 and the victory of the Welshman Henry
VII at Bosworth which effectively killed off political aspiration in
Wales itself for three or four centuries – even after those events, an
opportunity could have been taken in Welsh cultural history. In quieter vein than Thomas's, the painter and poet David Jones wrote of
the nine-hundred-year-long history of Wales's full nationhood from
A.D. 397 (when Cunedda entered the kingdom of Gwynedd from
Hadrian's Wall) to A.D. 1282. Jones saw the old Wales as profoundly rooted in Roman Britain and the Roman Empire, and, after
the Romans' departure, resulting in something "of which it will
never be possible not to take account in understanding Britain".
David Jones's Catholic temper and his less passionate political
stance seem to have let him feel that this is enough for Welsh pride,
so that he could be equable about the place of modern Wales. The
specifically political cause did not awaken him as it did Thomas. But
Thomas too, one remembers, was someone of considerable literary,
scriptural, liturgical and classical learning. He acknowledged his literary debts to the (English) Elizabethan age, to Shakespeare and
Donne, and he edited Herbert. And there are two highly relevant
references to be made here.

First, if surprisingly, there are more than passing echoes of
Matthew Arnold in *The Bread of Truth*, notably the Arnoldian short
regular and somewhat melancholic line in 'Song', 'So', 'Tramp',
'Welcome', 'Movement' and 'The Mill' with an explicit reference to
Arnold at the end of 'Song' and a clear echo at the end of 'The
Survivors', which immediately follows. This is more relevant to this
present discussion than it may seem. It was Arnold who attacked
what he saw as the dingy, philistine world of the chapel in *Culture
And Anarchy* with an energetic and biting satirical force similar to
that of the anonymous Kierkegaard, and with which, one imagines,
R.S. Thomas could identify as he did with Kierkegaard too. In that
book Arnold declared that Protestantism did not absorb the
Reformation nearly as much as was desirable if Britain were to have
developed a culture based on harmony and beauty, or – in Arnold's
famous phrase from that book and which is the quotation referred
to above which Thomas uses – "sweetness and light". It may even
be – I do not know – that Thomas found more in Arnold's well-
known testimony to the value of Celtic literature than many other
Welsh people have done.

Second, there is Thomas's introduction to his edition of Herbert.

This is dated 1967, right in the middle of the period we are talking about. In it Thomas makes a remark which is not quoted nearly often enough, if it is Thomas's views we are to understand. Having defended Herbert's relevance for the modern world, Thomas goes on to declare that Anglicanism, of all things, has the power still to provide the modern world with a consciously accepted discipline. "For many today [such a] discipline is equated with communism, socialism, humanism. Could it not as well or even better be Anglicanism?" On the face of it this is a most surprising remark. How can the staunch defender of a wholly independent Wales avow the central importance, for all social life, of the English established church, with its political preferments and, until relatively recently, its power? Even more remarkable is that the foundation of this English church as Reformed did not occur until the reign of Henry VIII, that is *after* the establishing of the Tudor dynasty, after the battle of Bosworth itself.

There seems to be a deep complexity here, in the middle of which however may be found Thomas's own true "cultural wound" to which R.M. Jones referred. It is my speculation of course; yet one wonders whether during the mid-sixties Thomas was not yearning, either unconsciously or in stoical silence, for a culture and its language rooted in the church he would have wished, in a different world and different history, to be at the heart of Wales. The Roman church reformed as, not now the Anglican, but the episcopal church in Wales, would have centred its worship on liturgy and sacrament, leading to the same cultural enrichment that pertained in Elizabethan England, with its Cranmer liturgy, its King James bible, its devotional poetry and its secular literature. But it would not have been English; it would have been Welsh, with its scripture and liturgy in the Welsh language; ritualistic, but in the Welsh language and of Welsh culture. The inference is that the Methodist revival would not have occurred, nor would the 'rescuing' of Welsh and the eighteenth-century 'invention' of the phony Welsh past which Thomas so often berates. One often senses in fact that Thomas simply had no interest in those things. Next to the real earlier moment of missed opportunity, they are latter-day, part of "worrying the carcase of an old song". It is, then, not surprising that the dismissal of the Welsh and Wales as political entities was so black and total. It is because it is all over. It is far too late.

It is this feeling that would seem to be at the root of Thomas's bitterest responses on the matter of the Welsh language. This is why he does not even deign to name the intruder, the "fat, monoglot stranger", by name. Nor is there any poem on any cultural of political event (with 'Loyalties' the one possible exception), or on Welsh cultural institutions or their activities; nor did such poems follow on the 1970s referendum on devolution, or any "praise poem" on any date of Welsh significance. No political stratagem is offered, no rallying manifesto. It is clearly the strong muscle of the language that remains important and its decline most ironic.

Nearly all Thomas's poems of Wales in *The Bread of Truth* are on the language. Some are sharp at the (unnamed) English:

> You have not been here before.
> You will offend with your speech
> Winds that preferred hands
> Wrung with despair, profound
> Audiences of the dead.
>
> ('Strangers')

One or two, like 'A Country', accuse the Welsh:

> the land
> Had no more right to its name
> Than a corpse had; self-given wounds
> Wasted it. It lay like a bone
> Thrown aside and of no use
> For anything except shame to gnaw.

But the most fulsome and desperate statement embroils his own predicament:

> I can't speak my own
> Language – Iesu,
> All those good words;
> And I outside them...
> I want my own
> Speech, to be made
> Free of its terms.
> I want the right word
> For the gut's trouble...
> I want the town even,
> The open door

Framing a slut,
So she can speak Welsh
And bear children
To accuse the womb
That bore me.

('Welsh')

The repetition of "want" plays on its double meaning, and to "want the town even ", from this poet, is to concede a lot.

But if Thomas really was cut off from the speech he most of all desired, he had little to add. Thomas strongly influenced the campaigns of the Welsh Language Society (*Cymdeithas Yr Iaith Gymraeg*) in the later nineteen sixties, and not without success; but his poetic effort is aborted. He could do no more on that front. There is little on the matter in *Pietà*, and by the time of *Not That He Brought Flowers* nothing remains but to write off the attempt, and the country. First, two comparisons with Welsh historical figures, Sir Gelli Meurig and Traeth Maelgwn, show their twentieth-century counterparts in a very unfavourable light. Like the ill-advised Elizabethan the modern Welsh "helplessly...dance/To a mad tune, who at home/ In the bracken could have remained/Humble but free", while on the other hand Maelgwn "kept his power/By intelligence; we lose/Ours for lack of it,/Holding our caps out/Beside a framed view/We never painted...". The "framed view" is reminiscent of the view Thomas himself sees more than once from his own windows, and which more than once moves him to comparison with great paintings, and to tears. Yet in the context of his antipathy to a Wales used only for the leisure of others, the emphasis is sometimes different. The acid contrast with Maelgwn was in the sphere of native intelligence, but in 'Reservoirs' a more full-bodied disgust is evident:

There are places in Wales I don't go...
The serenity of their expression
Revolts me, it is a pose
For strangers, a watercolour's appeal
To the mass, instead of the poem's
Harsher conditions.

In mock-obeisance to visiting royalty, presumably the Prince of Wales, the irony is wintry indeed:

> The prince walks upon the carpet
> Our hearts have unrolled
> For him; a worn carpet,
> I fear. We are a poor
> People; we should have saved up
> For this; these rents, these blood stains...
>   ('Loyalties')

To make out that Welsh "hearts" pay such homage might be very telling, suggesting there is no excuse, or dignity held in quiet reserve. On the other hand the worn carpet might be deliberately all that is offered. Either way the plays on "poor" and "rents" point even more accurately to what is happening in Thomas's writing itself. A celebratory literature does not sacrifice its language's richness to such internal rupture, and the poet uses this device to such an extent of black negation that it can be taken no further. We know that the dismissal of his country's hopes is complete. This occurs to saturation in a poem that has become notorious, 'Welcome to Wales':

> Come to Wales
> To be buried; the undertaker
> Will arrange it for you.

But the twenty-two line poem ends as follows:

>   This is what
> Chapels are for; their varnish
> Wears well and will go
> With most coffins. Let us
> Quote you; our terms
> Are the lowest, and we offer,
> Dirt cheap, a place where
> It is lovely to lie.

The reader is left with the dubious pleasure of counting the undeniably skilful seven or eight double-meanings scattered across the lines.

In later books R.S. Thomas returns occasionally to Wales with a different attitude. The country becomes a spiritual realm, and the body he has crucified is resurrected in the light of a new and quiet love. But for the moment the poet is left writing in the language to which he feels such ambivalence.

As has often been said, the result is laconic, dry, understated. It is the very mode, in fact, of the English poets most in the eye of the reading public at that time. Presences in Thomas's early period were Wordsworth and Yeats, albeit deeply assimilated. Later, an apparent influence of Ted Hughes's *Crow* in Thomas's *H'm* has been noted by many. But a certain affinity in this present period with even Philip Larkin has not been noted. Yet something of Larkin's concerns with the supermarket crowd in a poem like 'Here' (*The Whitsun Weddings*), is present in Thomas's own greater revulsion, and in Thomas's poem on his parents there is a clear parallel with Larkin's 'Home Is So Sad':

> What should have gone on,
> Arrow aimed from a tried bow
> At a tried target, has turned back,
> Wounding itself
> With questions you had not asked.
>
> ('Sorry')

Larkin's final stanza on the same topic thinks wistfully of a missed hope, containing the line "A joyous shot at how things ought to be". There are elsewhere a few other echoes of the laconic-polite English poets of the fifties. This is not to say that Thomas consciously or otherwise imitates these poets. Rather he is responding to a general listless mood in Britain as a whole in ways like theirs, and does not, or not as much as usual, try to hide this. It is an interim patch, something of an impasse. Thomas fitfully echoes T.S. Eliot and the *Four Quartets*, and the aphorism "the way forward is the way back" is used twice. First, it occurs in the opening poem of *The Bread of Truth*, 'A Line from St David's', where the poet seems to anticipate his new laconic tone and has to bring himself back from his mental wanderings to the matter in hand. It was in recalling "Dewi/The water-drinker" (St David) that the poet thought "the way back/Is not so far as the way forward". In the second case, curiously but quite consistently as it turns out, Thomas is addressing his earlier other self. "Take heart, Prytherch", he begins, and it is a little sad, and "Take heart, Thomas" would appear to underlie. The poet knows how it is. But the Eliot resonance feels like the temporary insertion of a different voice:

> Between better
> And worse is no bad place

For a labourer, whose lot is to seem
Stationary in traffic so fast.
Turn aside, I said; do not turn back.
There is no forward and no back
In the fields, only the year's two
Solstices, and patience between.

('Aside')

Patience is a theme in *Pietà*, but in both these passages it is the "aside" that is notable. To stand a little aside, in space and time, has seemed a provisional expedient. Thomas once wryly remarked in an address to the Poetry Society, "I play a small pipe, a little aside from the main road. But thank you for listening". It is hardly an adequate position for a poet of the national voice, but Thomas's recognition of where he had come to on his spiritual and personal journey was, thereby, no less acute.

There is another feature of this period, Thomas sometimes seems deliberately to rewrite an earlier poem in his new thinned, ironic tone. Both 'Song' and 'Encounter' echo earlier poems, 'Death of a Poet' in *Poetry for Supper* and 'Affinity' in *Song at the Year's Turning* respectively; but three other poems seem quite purposely to place the poet back in mind of an earlier incident and retell it in the light of sad experience. Here is 'Welsh Border':

It is a dark night, but noisy.
Cars pass on the road,
Their lights dissect me.
In the fields are the trees,
Brushed by a few stars.
The owls are restless.
People have died here.
Good men for bad reasons,
Better forgotten.
Trees grow no arrows
For the dead, enlistment
Of memories is over.
The real fight goes on
In the mind; protect me,
Spirits, from myself.

Point by point the features of 'Welsh Landscape' are taken out, or made secular. Trees, owls, arrows, battle and the heritage itself become mere noted entities with no power now to stir, "better forgotten". And in 'Truth' R.S. Thomas goes back to the scene where the peasant works, just as in 'Absolution' years before he had returned to Prytherch seeking forgiveness. But the routinizing of the response this time, its flat, lifeless feel, is knowingly made clear at once:

> He was in the fields, when I set out.
> He was in the fields, when I came back.
> In between, what long hours,
> What centuries might have elapsed.
> Did he look up? His arm half
> Lifted was more to ward off
> My foolishness...

The peasant is given no stone altar or mystic twilight this time for his life of endurance to radiate against, It is just there, and its truth is without flesh, the "bare bone of life that I pick". Again we see the bone, like the tree and the mirror, beginning to grow toward its final place as one of Thomas's central symbols. In the sonnet 'This', Thomas openly admits that he and Prytherch have not experienced the meeting of minds which in 'Green Categories' he had dared see occurring between the peasant and the philosopher Kant:

> I thought, you see, that on some still night,
> When stars were shrill over his farm,
> And he and I kept ourselves warm
> By an old fire...
>   the truth might ripen...

But it did not.

A number of other poems in this period seem to stand out by their formality. Perhaps the clearest examples are the title poem of the book *Not That He Brought Flowers*, and the earlier surprising and very beautiful poem 'Mrs Li', where profound longings for a quite different aspect of life seem to be at work:

> Mrs Li, whose person I adore,
> Said to me once, walking on the shore,
> The wind's voices whispering at the ear's
> Innocent portal: Love is like the sea's
> Wandering blossom; we are the waves,
> Who wear it wreathed a moment in our hair.

But I replied, toying with the sand
That was the colour of her carved hand,
Though warmer, veined more freely with the sun's
Tropical gold: No, love is like the sea's
Measureless music; we are the shells,
Whose lips transpose it to a brief despair.

The real or sublimated suggestion of "adultery already in your heart"
is justified by its exotic setting and by the balance of ways in which
love finds its image; the sea's innocence as flowers for the one, and
its despair as music for the other. Yet that despair has gone calm, a
moment's relief from the pain by forming a beauty from it which still
leaves it very real indeed. One feels all the poet's bitterness and pain
easing out through this relief, and a beautiful woman and scene
enabling it. The other important feature of this poem is its direct
source in Wallace Stevens. Thomas has already echoed Stevens in
earlier poems, notably 'Winter Starlings' in *Tares*, but here the influence is fuller. Thomas's own poem on Stevens, which appears only
a few pages after this one in *The Bread of Truth*, has a more partial
cast, in that it ignores the comedy and gaiety usually attributed to
Stevens. But 'Mrs Li' is so clearly an antiphonal poem to Stevens's
'To The One Of Fictive Music', that one feels Thomas's acknowledged exploring of Stevens during this period and half-hoping to find
the direction he so desperately wants. Twice in this period Thomas
writes poems on Kierkegaard, a philosopher with whose very
wracked, acid and fervid writing the poet has clearly found an identity too. But with Stevens I feel Thomas senses an opportunity. The
sensuous qualities Thomas finds at times almost unbearably in matter
itself, can be lifted forward into the poetry that would – as Stevens
himself once put it – "suffice". But Thomas has not the same formal
and equable philosophical temperament as Stevens, such that an
overall poetic philosophy could emerge from several poems, including (as with Stevens, and Eliot and Yeats too) very long ones. In 'Mrs
Li' R.S. Thomas finds a temporary equation which is lovely. But he
is also drawn to the brink of the physical which is expressed as nearly
irresistible, so that the "toying with the sand/That was the colour of
her carved hand" almost make the sand and hand unite.

In these rather separate and set poems the metaphor becomes
one with the poem. 'Shrine at Cape Clear' is another one. But usually in these three books the characteristically impressive Thomas
metaphors sit inside the poem, as though they too are a brief

"aside". In this period the poet turns again and again a new way, and the vivid metaphor now isolated in something linguistically thinner is one of them. The poem 'The Face' begins:

When I close my eyes, I can see it,
That bare hill with the man ploughing,
Corrugating that brown roof
Under a hard sky.

It is a brilliant image and an acute physical comparison. Again the poet cannot resist telling us about the act of seeing itself. There are several of these isolated metaphors in this period. There is Puw "opening his slow lips like a snail", the heart that like a bell "in its bone belfry hangs and is dumb" (from 'The Belfry', one of the book's outstanding poems), and the dying sailor in hospital – the poet's father – who "drifted/Away on the current/ Of his breath, further and further,/Out of hail of our love". But we must ask all the more, what do these isolated metaphors achieve? We have looked at the matter generally already, but now the question is of what they are doing in this period. If it is true that, in general, metaphor in poetry is an end in itself, something that teleologically we may even say we live for, then in these poems it seems that metaphor alleviates distress, and fills in the blank and bare. This is particularly caught by a metaphor Thomas uses more than once in this period, that of wind or fishing-rod "creasing" the water. That is to say, the blank surface of boredom is broken with a mark on it, perhaps the mark of rich metaphor itself. This brings us to the matter of what Thomas is really left with, what he is really writing about in these books. The only subject on which the poet's attention is direct and lasting is the matter of Wales, and we have seen how that ended. What else is there?

Prytherch gradually fades into the background. This is explicit in 'Servant', where the poet seems to imply, though with gratitude, that the need the peasant met has dissolved. "You served me well, Prytherch" the poet affirms, and then unforgettably elaborates it:

From all my questionings and doubts;
From brief acceptance of the times'
Deities; from ache of the mind
Or body's tyranny, I turned,
Often after a whole year,

> Often twice in the same day,
> To where you read in the slow book
> Of the farm, turning the fields' pages
> So patiently, never tired
> Of the land's story...

Yet the poet goes on to declare that this was not "the whole answer", and asks whether the truth is not wider, both enabling choice and imposing it, "with a clear eye and a free hand,/From life's bounty". But if Prytherch has served his purpose, what then becomes the object of the poet's fixed stare at the Other, so clearly marked in the first period of writing?

In *Not That He Brought Flowers*, there is some indication that this compulsion to see people one at a time is now being diversified, and this is a way forward. 'Careers', 'The Observer', 'Wedlock', 'The Fisherman', 'Sailors' Hospital', 'Touching' and others all have this tendency. It is no longer just the peasant who is looked at, for there are all manner of people. 'The Observer' as its title suggests, is the most explicit. The poet visits a mentally defective girl in a mental institution, and is led to ask himself about life's purposes. "How should I know/Its motives, who was not born/To question them, only to see/What I see...?" But instead of reaching out a poetic hand to these others in relationships that become transcendent (as happened with Prytherch), Thomas ends with generalities about deformed, limited and suffering people across the face of humanity. That is to say, he is left with no I-Thou relationship, to use Martin Buber's term. As a result there is nowhere to turn but to his own self, to see what each particular experience has done to his own consciousness and pain.

In 'This', cited earlier, a sad confession that minds did not meet after all, the poet makes clear that this is no longer even attempted:

> Keeping my own
> Company now, I have forsaken
> All but this bare basement of bone,
> Where the one dry flame is awake.

In both 'Careers', about Thomas's own son, and in 'Wedlock', about a farmer but one seen much more as participant in the world of technologized agriculture, Thomas is led to inturned thinking, to reflection:

He is out late at night
In the landrover...he is up before me
At raw tasks. Out in his hard cab
Of noise he invests the morning
With purpose...
                    Would I exchange
My life?

The question sits oddly and is not developed. Rather the farmer is seen not unlike Tomos in 'The Airy Tomb' as dogged and mute, concerned with an absent girl and her mother; or perhaps his own, so cryptic and dry is the poet's rendering. We see how Thomas is drawn into apprehension of a wider network of human contacts, in which those individuals neither impinge on himself repetitively in the poetry, nor do they belong to the world of each other. It is a woman who visits him, a tramp, a peasant, his son, a fisherman, a passing tourist, another peasant, and so on. Imaginatively, they have nothing to do with each other, except in his own consciousness. He must therefore question this consciousness itself, as to its own nature; and because it is thus solitary, "keeping my own company now", it is also the place for a wider questioning, often very painful, about reality generally, the experienced world.

The presence of the subjective self, the 'I', is thus very marked in this period. The objective world, the people or things stared at, has become dispersed. This is the result both of the gradual disappearance of Prytherch, but also the end of seeing the natural world in the old sacramental way, and without incorporating new technologized, existential experience. Many poems lean heavily on the first person, "I am sending you this letter...I ramble; what I wanted to say". ('A Line from St David's'); "I know those places and the lean men,as I go by,/I hear them pacing..." ('Country Cures'); "I can see their shapes", I can hear them speak" ('On the Shore'); "Move with the times?/I've done that all right" ('Movement'); "I praise you because/I envy your ability." ('Because'); "I see them walking/Up long streets" ('Blondes'); "There are places where I have not been/...I preferred Dragort" ('A Grave Unvisited'); "I know the reason/They cry..." ('They'). And finally, in the last poem in the last book of this period, after boredom has been registered as a conclusion, Thomas is watching the housemartins round his rectory, and records how he responds to them:

              my method is so
To have them about myself
Through the hours of this brief
Season and to fill with their
Movement, that it is I they build
In and bring up their young
To return to
                        ('The Place')

But the poet is far from merely self-centred. Again, it is a Protestantism threatening to go secular, and he finds the self is temporarily at least all he is left with. In two poems near the start of *Pietà*, 'This To Do' and 'Within Sound of the Sea', the poet faces squarely this strong pressure of the self needing a direction, a way. In both cases the sea is the context for this expression (Eglwysfach is in the Dyfi valley north of Aberystwyth near the west coast of Wales). In the first poem the poet takes an imaginative commitment one day to go down into the sea's depths "to search for the door/To myself", risking a lack of breath to do it, while in the second poem the picture is a more literal one of the poet's day to day life, in which as a country vicar he can read for long hours, but is always conscious of the sea-shore close by and his own desire to walk by it, to visit the "caged beast" it embodies. This is a very exposed poem, one of the most candid Thomas has written. It leads, as in a rush, to many questions for which in hindsight we feel we have been waiting:

                    What does it mean,
That I have the power to do this
All day long if I wish to?
I know what thoughts will arise,
What questions. They have done so before,
Unanswered...

As a result, a deeper theme of this period emerges. Taken from the obdurate physical world into the existential world, the poet experiences questioning as a normal state. It is not this or that question as such that haunts him, although many of course do. But there is a further feeling on the reader's part, that these probes, asides and sometimes hurtful experiences (as in 'Please' and 'This'), the temptations at times to return such hurts with a gracelessness himself – all of these are only incidental circlings round the central condition.

They were asked as though publicly; they constituted the poem's thrust and the reader was left with them. In this later period (although it began to move in this direction before the end of *Tares*), the questioning feels more inward and part of a general perplexity. This perplexity in its turn seems more than a search after reality's nature. The question is sometimes why what he sees is there at all. Of a funeral, "What have they come here to mourn?" ('Funeral'). Of holiday-makers, "What have they come here to find?" ('Resort'). Of farmers who lived in the hills, toiled and died, "Why did they do it?" ('The Mill'). Thomas, walking by the sea, even asks, "What is the beach for?" ('On The Shore'). There are further questions of a religious nature, and about the perplexity itself, but, since they are always left as questions without answers, questioning itself is left as the mode of address in the world the poet inhabits.

Part of Protestantism's approach to reality is a tendency to strip life down to a single dimension, or order, or correlative. The orthodox Protestant has not the trappings of polytheism or the full emphasis on the varied rites and ceremonies of other churches. The Protestant is thus left with a revealed truth or story in scripture, and with his or her own conscience or direct communication from a strongly authoritative and monotheistic god. When this tradition finds itself in a secular and existential world, it gropes about for some single entity to replace or update that original mythic formulation. Without it, the original spiritual energy is likely to be redirected in an equally single focus on social action, such as a creed like socialism itself, or a cause within that, or a protest against whatever social organization pertains. R.S. Thomas certainly evinces some of these characteristics. The compulsive staring at the single peasant, and the championing of an independent Wales, and strong disgust when that cause seems to fail, are two dissimilar examples of the single tendency. But a strongly religious sensibility in the same conditions will need some further dimension as well. In two poems in this period Thomas confronts this 'questioning' directly, and in both cases he is in the wholly natural world, with the appurtenances of human invention scarcely present. In both these poems, furthermore, asking the universal question also calls up some deeper presence along with it, some spirit or consciousness fused through the natural world. In 'So', a strange, elusive, mythic poem with Arnoldian echoes, a voice of unnamed source is postulated from which

> Phrase by phrase there formed
> The old reply to the earth's
> Question; the lips affirmed
>
> With tired patience the worth
> Of bird and flower, appealed
> To vows made at his birth.

The poem is inconclusive. At the end the "weak glance failed/To travel to the far hill", but we do not know whose glance it is, and the patience of whatever spoke was "tired". Nevertheless that universal question, and the sense of it, are postulated. In a later poem, 'Amen', Thomas seems at last to have reached some formula adequate to his present condition. The entities present are no more realized in any graspable detail (though God is named), yet the affirmation is strong and the result therefore positive:

> And God said; How do you know?
> And I went out into the fields
> At morning and it was true.
>
> Nothing denied it, neither the bowed man
> On his knees, nor the animals,
> Nor the birds notched on the sky's
>
> Surface. His heart was broken
> Far back, and the beasts yawned
> Their boredom. Under the song
>
> Of the larks, I heard the wheels turn
> Rustily. But the scene held;
> The cold landscape returned my stare;
>
> There was no answer. Accept; accept.
> And under the green capitals,
> The molecules and the blood's virus.

Because the bare scene is finally and wholly confronted, and the question of questions faced, acceptance is reached. The result is a sudden attention, in the poem's last two lines, to the much closer particularities seen through the scientist's microscope. Thomas can begin to prepare for later interests. But the present condition by which acceptance of question as question-with-no-answer has occurred is a broad, empty scene. And it is this very breadth and bareness which, at first, make the only possible universe for Thomas's religious apprehensions in an unreligious world.

This bareness is something Thomas himself often confirmed, outside of his poetry, that he deeply valued. It is irreducible in its nature, in that it is without distracting detail whether scientific, economic, domestic or political; and it is the background against which Thomas chose to live his own life. In 'The Minister', the moor hung empty but large, seeming to possess truth the chapel congregation ignored or missed. Now in 'The Moor', which is one of Thomas's best known poems from this period, there is something of a religious drawing-near:

> It was like a church to me.
> I entered it on soft foot,
> Breath held like a cap in the hand.
> It was quiet.

It is so appealing and approachable because at least for a time the poet is satisfied. This bareness Thomas so needs is found in many parts of nature; on the moor, in sky and the birds that fly there, in the sea and in the world of the seamen who have travelled it world-wide, and, more unusually in this context, in the church building itself, which Thomas so often apprehends in its emptiness. It is the absence of boundary, of distinction, that seems to appeal. In 'Swifts' the poet gives himself entirely to a meditation which is pleasurable and perplexing at once:

> Sometimes they glide,
> Or rip the silk of the wind
> In passing. Unseen ribbons
> Are trailing upon the air.
> There is no solving the problem
> They pose, that had millions of years
> Behind it, when the first thinker
> Looked at them.

Two breath-taking metaphors of insubstantiality itself, but the expansiveness the poet needs is found here in time past, as well as in space. In 'Ravens' the birds occupy similar boundlessness; "They

had all air/ To themselves." In 'The Survivors' the poet equally loses
himself in an outside narrative. In the poems about the church we
touch on a different matter, which Thomas will elaborate in its theological implications far more in later books. For the present, the
attempt is to find bareness itself as an attribute of the church building, as though to wall in space with "stones...wrenched/From the
moorland", a phrase from the poem 'There', in which it is again the
long-suffering farmers who are only too relieved to give thanks to
God for the tiniest gains in their lifelong struggle. But in 'In Church'
Thomas grapples at some length with the emptiness itself, with a
notable conclusion. He begins:

> Often I try
> To analyze the quality
> Of its silences. Is this where God hides
> From my searching? ...
>   It has waited like this
> Since the stones grouped themselves about it.

That is to say, the emptiness itself, in effect a small square
yardage of the moorland air, has been netted, to incubate a greater
spiritual intensity. But the emptiness is finally compounded by
another one:

> There is no other sound
> In the darkness but the sound of a man
> Breathing, testing his faith
> On emptiness, nailing his questions
> One by one to an untenanted cross.

So the central icon of Christianity itself is empty too. And this now
leads us on to a way by which to see what this bareness is for
Thomas, and how it takes him to his later, final religious search.

In the title poem, 'Pietà', the same adjective is employed:

> And in the foreground
> The tall Cross,
> Sombre, untenanted,
> Aches for the Body
> That is back in the cradle
> Of a maid's arms.

Alongside the blackest negation toward the church itself yet expressed, in 'The Belfry' ("the heart/In its bone belfry hangs and is dumb"), these two poems open the door, if only slightly, to Thomas's only way back to making some sense of his religion's chief tenets in their orthodox form. We have emphasized the bareness which is the locus of this questioning itself, the very stance of questioning. But there is usually a far more ominous quality in the references to the empty, free, wide and bare than we have yet suggested.

In 'Then', Thomas is out on the moor again, this time not alone. But the ending is far from a conventionally sacramental one:

> Nothing that nature
> Did was a contradiction
> That time, and the prey hung
> Jewels of blood round the day's throat.

It is chilling, the more so because it seems intentionally pleasurable. Despite the killing, "nothing that nature did was a contradiction that time", even though in the usual image to which Thomas has recourse, they had "wandered upon the broad hills'/Back, crumbling the air's/Poetry". This is the new note we are now hearing. In a very different poem, one of the few occasional poems Thomas wrote on the matter of Wales but which, again, centres on himself, he contrasts the civic flower-beds of London with something far wilder:

> I am not one
> Of the public; I have come a long way
> To realise it. Under the sun's
> Feathers are the sinews of stone,
> The curved claws.
>   ('A Welshman At St James' Park')

The occasion, though it is only my guess, was surely when Thomas paid a rare visit to London in 1964 to receive the Queen's Gold Medal for poetry. The poet's preference remains evident, nonetheless, for "the curved claws" over "birds/That have been reduced from wildness by/ Bread they are pelted with."

This contrast between the ordered garden and the untamed and cruel wilderness surfaces in a number of poems of this period. It begins to seem significant and pressing. 'The Garden' and 'The Untamed' are two of the most obvious examples. The import of

'The Untamed' is unequivocal. The poet's wife prefers the sheltered enclosure; the poet prefers the wild. He acknowledges that the formal garden has peace of a kind, but not "the deep peace/Of wild places". That kind of peace he was later to say, in 'The Moor', brought "stillness/Of the heart's passions". But the alternative is the passionless cruelty of the bird and beast of prey. There is no doubting the thrust of this poem, for the poet quite deliberately adopts a stance different from that of conventional care of the vulnerable. He admits his wife's care enables the weaker plants to get their needed nourishment and air, but still goes straight on that "Despite my first love,/I sometimes take her hand". One must either read "first" as chronological, or more likely take it that Thomas is leading the reader into deeper, darker paths. Again the poet ends with a palpably frightening image. He allows that the garden tames "the wild hawk of the mind" temporarily, "But not for long", for "I stoop/Here only in play". The hawk stoops to its prey, we have another double meaning, and the cruelty of nature is seen as possessing the dreadful dimension of blood sport.

This most honest of poets is, then, unafraid to acknowledge the libido of the primitive blood-lust in himself. It appears again in three poems he has published, in this period, about a visit to Spain. The most disturbing, I feel, is 'Coto Donana', given here in full because of the various things symptomatic of this matter that it contains:

> I don't know; ask the place.
> It was there when we found it:
> Sand mostly, and bushes, too;
> Some of them with dry flowers.
> The map indicates a lake;
> We thought we saw it from the top
> Of a sand-dune, but walking brought it
> No nearer.
>   There are great birds
> There that stain the sand
> With their shadows, and snakes coil
> Their necklaces about the bones
> Of the carrion. At night the wild
> Boars plough by their tusks'
> Moonlight, and fierce insects
> Sing, drilling for the blood
> Of the humans, whom time's sea
> Has left there to ride and dream.

There is no pity, no justification. The first line has an ennui, one which surfaces more than once among the poems where this one is published, toward the end of *Not That He Brought Flowers*. Then the weird experience of the receding lake – which the present writer has known too on occasion – prepares one for a world beyond reason: yet, when that comes, it is even more surprising after the previous phrase's hesitation. The sudden, irresistible surge of the monosyllables ("there are great birds/There") as though a pent-up primitive thirst is being exposed to the daylight, the way the second "there" rounds to the first, and how the alliteration in "stain the sand" makes such a very perceptive image even more forceful; the onomatopoeic sibilants in the presentation of the insects, followed by the different and ominous sound of the "drilling", which is the passage's key word, with the sound of the 'I' seeming nearly to evoke the actual smell of "blood" – all of this emanates from a sensibility which is willing to permit a savagery to be expressed, which most ordinary people no doubt have and suppress in equal proportions. A good many more of Thomas's poems have this power; it was vibrant in 'Welsh Landscape' many years before, and it concludes 'Burgos', one of the other Spanish poems and one of the very last poems of this period.

It leads, directly, to the crucifixion. That at least seems to be Thomas's inference, and while he has no doubt worked it out in the logical dimension too, logic is not the original experience. For this particular Welsh Christian, the crucifixion was the more relentlessly necessary the more one faces the nature of the primitive sacrifice that is demanded by the blood lust that humans apparently have. No intervention from a god who would defeat evil by love could be taken seriously unless the evil itself is taken seriously; no costless reference to 'problems', or a conventional list of forms of anti-social behaviour, could make a modern reader do anything other than consign the Jesus-crucifixion story to the garbage-can of all such earlier blood sacrifices that an advanced civilization, presumably, wants to leave behind. Thomas takes the story seriously by evoking what he feels in himself. It is possibly for this reason, too, that while the poems on peasants decline in this period (there are nine, six and three respectively in the three books) a certain quiet tenderness in them replaces the more outward anger at the peasant's toil that characterized the earlier period. And this too culminates in the later part of *Not That He Brought Flowers*, in the poem 'They', where this rigorously unsentimental poet rarely acknowledges a physical contact:

> I take their hands,
> Hard hands. There is no love
> For such, only a willed
> Gentleness....

The tenderness cannot be an indulgence, because by now it contrasts an impulse that is frightening.

The Cross then is "untenanted", in that it is bare and empty, and that appeals to the primitive impulse. It comes furthermore out of nature, for it is a tree with Thomas's equally loved bird in its branches. This image appears in a poem at the end of this period ('That'), and again the nailing of the suffering individual is entailed. One begins to see a meaning in the many comparisons of tree with peasant in *Song at the Year's Turning*. Thomas's theology has no Easter, no ascension, and even the joyous season of Christmas points, for believers, nowhere but forward with (at the Christmas communion service) "the sharp taste/Of blood they will shed."

But this primitive, savage impulse is also associated with boredom. In this later part of this third book it is evident in 'Study', 'That' ("this blank indifference...") and 'Again', as well as in the different contexts of 'Resort' and 'Commuters'. And in 'Again', the second main story of traditional theology that magnetizes Thomas so much in later books begins to insinuate itself:

> What to do? It's the old boredom
> Come again: indolent grass,
> Wind creasing the water
> Hardly at all; a bird floating
> Round and round. For one hour
> I have known Eden...

The loved bird is uninteresting for once, and the stimulating rupture so often found in the wind "creasing" the water now happens "hardly at all". The scene, it seems, is again a garden, described earlier in the poem of that name as "the old kingdom of man" (that is, Eden itself), in which "the buds come" as "power wielded without sin". That is to say, they are not yet wrongs advanced enough to be catalogued by a theological law, but again the naked predatory impulse of our nature itself. And this brings a further aspect of this period into focus. For this second aspect of Thomas's theology which will be expanded in *H'm* and after, the Garden of Eden, is latently present, in this second period, in Thomas's attitudes to origin, sex and family.

We noted that Prytherch recedes. In his place comes the family of the Puws. They have not even Prytherch's ignorant fumblings toward reason and light. To put it in the classical terms Thomas knows as well as well as do most contemporary poets, it is the primitive world of Aeschylus rather than the epistemological one of Sophocles. The wretched Puws are on the bottom rung of the evolutionary ladder, and it was Puw who was ironically named, representing his family, as greatest contrast to the prince who represents the visiting royal family in 'Loyalties'. These Puws are not merely at the bottom; the prospect of evolution is not even open to them:

> There was Dai Puw. He was no good.
> They put him in the fields to dock swedes,
> And took the knife from him, when he came home
> At late evening with a grin
> Like the slash of a knife on his face.
>   ('On the Farm')

The grin as the knife-wound again exemplifies Thomas's characteristic metaphoric touch. A smile and a knife gash have no right to be compared in a sensible world. Dai Puw's brothers are equally stuck. In 'Gospel Truth' they evince a little more imagination, but it is warped and weird. Matthew Puw has some capacity to organize, but is possessed of a savage violence. Mark Puw's mind is the embodiment of whining and complaint, but Luke Puw has hallucinations and is mad. But in both these poems, as well as in 'Brothers', there is one woman. It is apparently a sister, wife or necessary female in the first two poems, and in 'Brothers' it is the mother who is "rambling on interminably as the wind". In both the other two poems the girl appears last, speaking some strange or twisted message, as though she is the medium of whatever life force or dark power gives her brothers their existence. This element is the key to the poems and their directing symbol. The woman in Thomas's poetry is the fatal cause of reproduction and of origin itself, just as Eve is held both to have fallen to the temptation of the serpent, to carnal desire, and to have led Adam into the same fall. Thomas seems profoundly suspicious, even afraid, of this originary power. It would be superficial merely to call it 'sex' with all of our modern connotation wrapped into that term, although in the poems about the trashy young girls and sluts (sic) of modern existence the sexual implication is clear enough. But one senses that, to Thomas, this is more than merely a moral sin of desire uncontrolled. The result of uncontrolled sex is uncontrolled birth.

This is a deeper horror for the poet than any lasciviousness. Unlike Prytherch, the Puws make a family; too many, unnecessary progeny. Women of nubile age pose a threat to males, symbolized repeatedly by hair, the bodily feature the poet names far more than any other. 'Blondes' are young girls whose hair characterizes them; a Welsh sailor took a girl who "caught him in her thin hair" ('The Boy's Tale'); rivals at Catraeth contended for a woman "in her downpour of hair" ('Ravens'); Kierkegaard too, who in great sadness denied himself a young wife for her own sake, felt "her hair was to be/The moonlight towards which he leaned/ From darkness" ('Kierkegaard'). And the poet, too, recognizes the survival of his own sexual proclivities after middle age when dance or disco move him closer in than usual. He puns ruefully ("the dry rut of age"), but can still feel the yearnings: "Let me smell/My youth again in your hair" ('The Dance'). In more sublimated fashion the beloved Mrs Li feels the sea's "wandering blossom" is "wreathed a moment in our hair", and the poet is left toying with the sand and the possibility. In 'Female' in *H'm* the smell of Eve's hair drives Adam crazy. Hair has the dangerous power to ensnare and entwine. For the poet, actual touching is like an electric contact, as in 'Touching' where "It is the man burns". In both this poem and 'The Visit' a hardly concealed anger is the response to the apparently older woman's subtler proximity; for, after her own anger at him, "she rose,/Touched the tips of my cold/Hand with hers and turned/To the closed door. I remember/Not opening it."

Thomas's own sexual urges as a man are never denied by him. They occur in his own personal poems (in the middle of 'Marged' in *Laboratories Of The Spirit* we get a rare glimpse of where he might be vulnerable), as well as those on modern life or the Garden of Eden story. But the implication is wider. The matter is encapsulated in one poem, 'Parent', evidently about Adam and Eve themselves, though they are not named. "So he took her – just like that", the poem begins; yet this all too easy liaison gave rise to "the loading/Of that huge womb" and

> the whole earth
> A confusion of persons,
> Each with his grudge
> Rooted in the enormous loins
> Of the first parent.

Certain poems about his own parents, and later ones evincing something of a sad curiosity about his father, show Thomas under personal burdens which have enlarged his emotional stance on the matter. Again Thomas's autobiographical prose statements support these suggestions. In the poems on his own family we repeatedly feel the profound care – in two senses – that is incumbent on the individual who would not be ensnared in the whole human lot in this respect. 'Exchange', in its quiet way, is a deep tribute to his wife, and in 'Careers' there is a very tender, if sad, recognition of what it is to bring one's own son into the world. Twice (in 'Anniversary' in *Tares* and in 'Gifts' in this period) he names hunger as the legacy the offspring is left in the nature of things, a hunger far more than physical. I feel that this second thrust in Thomas's own personal mythology of Christianity, the import of the Adam and Eve story, emerges deeply from his own experience, and is then diffused across the whole range of families, women and children he observes, and meets. In the end it is orthodox. The old Adam sinned, perhaps in Eden's boredom, but the carnal lust that irreversibly surfaced there is part of the wilder action impregnated across all nature and which thirsts for sacrifice, for blood. Somebody somewhere, no one yet named, must be nailed up on the tree to satisfy this blood lust, and that tree, "untenanted,/Aches for the Body...".

In fact, the curiously incomplete title of the third book, *Not That He Brought Flowers*, suggests this. So far, however, it is tentative. But two poems late in this period capture the feeling of a search for the fuller expression that is to come. In 'After the Lecture', as in 'Within Sound of the Sea', the language is surprisingly and unusually candid:

> I'm asking the difficult question. I need help.
> I'm not asking from ill-will...
> I've read your books...
> > I may have grown

> Since reading them; there is no scale
> To judge by, neither is the soul
> Measurable.

But in this particular poem the resulting question is only the immediate one of what good a priest's prayer is, who knows his role all too well and accepts it. It marks the end of the link between the poet and the pastoral clergyman. This link was explicit in 'The Country Clergy' (*Song at the Year's Turning*), 'Country Cures', and most fully 'The Priest'. In the latter, the priest sees himself and his colleagues accused of shielding themselves from the secular world by dwelling on the harsh and spiritual. The priest answers: " 'Let it be so', I say. 'Amen and amen.' "

But finally, in 'Kneeling', an often-quoted passage illustrates the more universal attitude the priest has to hold to for a long, if intermediary, time. He is in church again, this time with the congregation present and expectant, and he holds the moment steady. But what he says is only between himself and God:

> Prompt me, God;
> But not yet. When I speak,
> Though it be you who speak
> Through me, something is lost.
> The meaning is in the waiting.

The pastoral vicar moves perceptibly toward the mystic. The echo of Augustine merges with the necessary stance of a twentieth century man. Like Simone Weil and Beckett's tramps, for this period at least, Thomas waits.

III. God Absent and Present

(*H'm* 1972, *Laboratories of the Spirit* 1975, *Frequencies* 1978)

> God looked at space and I appeared,
> Rubbing my eyes at what I saw.
>
> ('Once')

So begins the first poem in *H'm*, and the couplet's eye-opening quality underlines that this is to be a period of poetic production very different from both the earlier ones. This period is clearly demarcated from the one before and *H'm* is a new start. In this third period the questioning is different. R.S. Thomas still asks questions, but chooses an identity about which and of which to ask them. This identity is God. The three books wrestle with, undermine, approach, accuse, despair of and affirm God. Unlike the previous period with its uncertainties, this period's clear subject is God.

Already this first poem shows a startling change. The persona behind the earlier periods never "appeared", as unexpectedly or unwittingly as that, and certainly never rubbed his eyes, either in surprise or from sleep. His stare was perpetual and unblinking. Equally, when we read below that "God spoke. I hid myself in the side/Of the mountain", it is difficult to feel the stern and static detachment of the earlier voice. Either the writer has developed in some way or the 'I' refers to someone else.

It is perhaps not important to find an identity for the speaker in this poem 'Once'. He might be taken as Adam, humanity or R.S. Thomas in a particular disposition. More significant is that it is a mythic narrative in which the speaker is apparently the object or result of some act of God, and yet knows this and can tell us so. This activating of the speaker, if that can be read from the poem, does not prevent the speaker having much cultural and natural knowledge at his disposal:

> As though born again
> I stepped out into the cool dew,

Trying to remember the fire sermon,
Astonished at the mingled chorus
Of weeds and flowers. In the brown bark
Of the trees I saw the many faces
Of life, forms hungry for birth,
Mouthing at me. I held my way
To the light, inspecting my shadow
Boldly; and in the late morning
You, rising towards me out of the depths
Of myself.

The speaker is apparently bewildered, but also curious, and has not simply come into existence at that moment for the first time. There is nothing, in fact, to prevent us calling her 'she', unless the biblical creation story, and Adam's rib, impose themselves more strongly. Generally, it seems that that story is being imaginatively joined with the numerous originary myths found at the centre of small and undeveloped cultures the world over. At the same time the poem is marked with a distinctly twentieth century note, in that the speaker is sophisticated enough to conceive of "forms hungry for birth" and, more explicitly, with the partner who arises out of him and is his companion, goes "forth to meet the Machine".

This first poem then is centred on the action of God, the first poem of the second book *Laboratories Of The Spirit* is an address to God, and the first word of the third book *Frequencies* is "God". What is happening is that R.S. Thomas has turned away from the real landscape near him, and attempts to render or evoke God in mythic mode though with a twentieth century orientation. The change of parish in 1967, and – even more – Thomas's attested disillusion with Welsh referendum-politics in these years, clearly lie behind his sharply different new emphasis. The poems give the orthodox Old Testament stories, but radically altered. This occurs in several poems. For example, Cain and Abel are named in 'Cain', and only very inverted readings could avoid the biblical and primitive-world reference in 'Echoes', 'Soliloquy', 'Repeat', 'Female' and others. In 'Soliloquy', for example, God says "I have blundered/Before; the glaciers erased/My error", thus invoking a very long time-span. And in 'The Coming' God talks to "the son" (twice mentioned, although not "his son"), showing him a small globe. Visible is a bare tree with people round it and with arms outstretched to it

as though waiting
For a vanished April
To return to its crossed
Boughs.

By the enjambment of "crossed" it is impossible to miss a reference
to the cross where Jesus was crucified, which is not to say that this
is a fixed allusion with no possible alternatives. In fact the poem
ends:

The son watched
Them. Let me go there, he said.

But, at the same time, there are differences from the Old
Testament story. God is in no way perfect, and he fails to embody
both total love and total power or knowledge. In 'Echoes' the God
speaks bad-temperedly, while in 'Soliloquy' God is an intellectual
being who, however, recognizes two or three clear cases of failure of
his arts or intellectual understanding. "I have blundered/Before...I
have forgotten/How long...I listened to you/ Too long". In 'Female'
God creates a woman, but the ensuing eroticism and her wiles omit
God from the resulting narrative. In 'Cain' God is challenged by
Cain, and forced to answer.

In the poem with the most clear-cut narrative line – that is, the
one the reader most has to take literally – God seems to embody a
wilful cruelty and nothing else. This poem is 'The Island', and it
consists of a list of declarations by God of what he intends to do, all
of dire consequence for the island's inhabitants. The poem is reminiscent of the Minotaur in ancient Greece, and the final line is the
only one in the poem not spoken by God: " And that was only on
one island...". In *Laboratories of the Spirit* this is modified to some
degree, in that in some poems such as 'The Hand' and 'The Tool'
there is greater attention to the implications of what God does, and
what as a result he cannot control. The poet's own voice intrudes on
the questioning, and affects each poem's later stages. But in 'Rough'
the god is as mechanically heartless as the god of 'The Island' is
cruel, and the difference lies only in a certain emotional emphasis
which seems to impregnate the poem from the poet. As a result of
a nursery-rhyme echo in the opening lines of 'Rough', an anger pervades the later evocations of the unpleasant in the made creature;
"blood and faeces", "an obscene/ question", "tears of pus".

Secondly, it is not clear in a number of these mythic poems what the elusive pronouns refer to. If "I" is Adam in 'Once' we are not told so, nor is the place – perhaps the earth or the Garden of Eden – named. It is not named in 'Echoes' either; rather, a characteristically physical evocation is offered, centred on a church-bell metaphor equally robust and palpable:

> What is this? said God. The obstinacy
> Of its refusal to answer
> Enraged him. He struck it
> Those great blows it resounds
> With still. It glowered at
> Him, but remained dumb,
> Turning on its slow axis
> Of pain, reflecting the year
> In its seasons.

Later birds and animals appear, in apparent contentment, along with an "absence" into which "the shapes came, slender/As trees, but with white hands,/Curious to build". In 'Repeat', man is named, but not God or earth, yet of the poem's "he" the conclusion is "It was not his first time to be crucified".

These mythic poems, then, seem to rewrite the creation stories, both through a twentieth century mode, and with a tendency too of the poet's own. They attempt to grapple with the matter of God by seeing to what extent God can direct narrative. It is also as though the poet is challenging the good God of Christianity to defy him. But, equally, it is as though the poet is trying out versions of the story to see whether the myth can hold our attention, or whether it can yield new resonances, and allow in twentieth century technological components, or even be altered so radically as to allow little of the original to remain theologically or ethically. In 'Other', for example, it is God's destructive act rather than man's that appears to take peace from the world; while in 'The Tool' it is God who has projected on to him the role of Adam, for "God/knew he was naked and/withdrew himself". "Withdrew" also has a double meaning; as the title dryly suggests.

But the biblical symbol that most gets rewritten is that of the wound in Christ's side. This becomes a new symbol of great significance. It is compounded with Adam's rib, and appears again and again in the poems as a wound in the side of God from the time of the creation or before, and in strange combinations with other parts of the created world. So "the sun was torn/from my side", as God says in 'Soliloquy'; and in 'God's Story' God "fingered the hole/in his side, where the green tree/came from". In 'Ann Griffith', remarkably, it is God, not the sinner, who says "I thirst, I thirst/for the spring water". All of these examples may be locally transliterated to yield a tenable meaning, but it does not seem that one could build a systematic interpretation from them. Rather, curious indirections and cryptic rearrangements are proliferated, as though to underline the living quality of the myth and its components. It suggests that, if this discourse has value, it is written in and through the language that presents it. Moreover, if the wound in the side can be so universalized, it becomes something of a rupture at the heart of existence itself, the very mark of identity. It is also the extremity of agony and pain. One feels the same insistence in the constant introduction of the tree, clearly the cross of the crucifixion story in many instances, but invoked on so many occasions that we become accustomed to reading that into it where it is not explicit. Moreover, it is almost invariably a tree to which somebody is "nailed", one of the most insistent verbs in the poetry of this period and these three books. Yet the one case where Thomas is briefly explicit about the tree's existence, the same rupture as of the wound is evoked:

> He had
> to be killed; salvation acquired
> by an increased guilt. The tree,
> with its roots in the mind's dark,
> was divinely planted. the original fork
> in existence.
>
> ('Amen')

"The original fork in existence", that is the metaphysical centre of what is said. It is possible to speculate that a new consciousness has developed in the poet through the rupture in his own poetic existence, marked by the change in subject, style (absence of capitals at the start of lines, etc) and other things. But this is not to imply his work has an overall disunity in the end. Rather, in placing weight on these two markings of the Old and New Testament stories, namely, the wound and the tree, Thomas is evoking matters which are at the heart of late twentieth century understanding of reality. Mathematics, anthropology, theology, linguistics and literary criticism are some modes where it is found. It may seem rather abstract and academic to raise such matters, but the poetry explores them again and again quite deliberately, and so this cannot be ignored.

The centre of modern computation, to take an unlikely seeming case, is the binary digit, simply the division of anything into two, mere bland unity divided. Contemporary theologians have given considerable attention to the significance for modern man of the same two stories. The question of the Fall of man as resulting from the division of man into two sexes ties in with Thomas's own deep doubts about origin and, perhaps, a desire for some primal unity, achievable (perhaps) in a longed-for Wales of the past or Abercuawg of the future. This is what the poem 'Abercuawg' suggests; namely, that place to which we may never come, so that it remains for ever the object of our desire. For the radical theologian John Hick, the problem of the Fall was traditionally resolved by saying that God created finite beings for fellowship with himself, and this necessitated their being at an "epistemic distance" from himself; once again, unity divided. There is therefore no need to wonder whether an all-powerful, all-loving God "willed" the Fall, for that does not arise. Thus, although Hick himself doubts whether the discourse is still serviceable, the story is not inconsistent with a modern evolutionary view of humanity. For it mythically underwrites specifically human evolution. The imprint of a rupture on a unitary beginning, in effect, was essential for identification of anything; that is to say, for anything to be different from anything else, and therefore for knowledge to grow. The literary critic Northrop Frye saw something analogous in the Fall, which did not so much cut humans off from God, as give them some kind of bodily knowledge (i.e. of sex and nakedness) which itself contained a binary mark, namely the distinction between good and evil, like Thomas's "original fork in existence" again. But, equally, the rupture must be a wound or an execution, since it is the source of evil and pain as well. Frye went on to refer to the tree of the crucifixion in terms similar to those of Thomas in 'Amen'. The tree is the mediaeval *axis mundi*, the earth's axis or vertical line going down through it, a feature now seen to be common in originary myths the world over. It seems quite clear that Thomas's repeated references to the tree, going back to *Song at the Year's Turning*, have been leading toward this basic symbol. The man 'nailed' to this tree is thus taken back to nature, no longer mobile but still vertical as befits the one erect creature.

Literary critics equally will see in the foregoing much of what has been suggested by the French philosopher Jacques Derrida, who sees difference as the condition of all sign or signification whatever, and thus of all writing. It is this connection with the act of writing which is important in the contemporary world, where, in fact, mythic explanations of origin are demythologized. Thomas is actually writing this rupture, updating the theological myth into the act of writing itself. Again and again in this period Thomas winds a poem round, away from and then back to the figure of the hole in the side, or the tree on which the body is nailed, or the paradisal place into which elusive, shadowy humans come. The farmer ploughs "under the tall boughs/Of the tree of the knowledge of/Good and evil" ('This One'). An opponent in religious dialectic pardons the speaker "Under the green tree/Where history nailed him" ('Parry'). He prays that "leaves/from the deciduous Cross/fall on us" ('The Prayer'); and in a subsequent poem he expands on that trope explicitly, declaring "the Cross an example/of the power of art to transcend timber". A man or body is nailed to a tree in 'Mediations', 'The Reception', 'Hill Christmas' and other poems. The many 'Garden of Eden' poems include 'Once', 'The Gap' (*Laboratories of the Spirit*), 'Echoes', and 'Making'. Variations on the hole in the side include the letting of blood from it, the removal and/or replacement of the bone", and the imputation of this to God, some other, or the poet himself. It occurs in 'Cain', 'Via Negativa', 'Soliloquy', 'The Hand', 'God's Story', 'The Prayer', 'Suddenly', 'The Interrogation', 'The Woman', 'Hesitations' and others. The way the figure is used in 'The Woman' shows, furthermore, that the poet has taken the symbol far further than its spare-rib connotation might have led one to expect; it is more general and metaphysical. If, in the world of this poetry, females are more than once painful to males, it is certainly not a prototype.

The general group of mythic poems is the initial step in the wider new departure of this period. As we have said already, many of these poems are in the first book *H'm*. They do not disappear, but the proportion dwindles, considerably so by the end of *Frequencies*. The question remains of their import. We have emphasized all along that Thomas is the poet of the strong metaphor, the succulent and vivid conjunction of two physical things with each other. But it is clear too that the whole period is targeted on God. If one is to write about God – that is to say, to articulate God, or what one feels about God, or even articulate God's own conceived mode of expression – it cannot be so direct. Whatever else God is, God has to be materially invisible, inaudible, untouchable. (John Milton himself had problems making his God-figure credible in *Paradise Lost*). It seems then that some special contrivance will be needed. And Thomas's first contrivance is to put the myth-stories to work as metaphors, in the hope that their metaphoric components would touch off other things from outside the myth – from the poet's own sensitivities to his physical world – and so make new and fruitful combinations.

Yet the result is more than that too. For if one keeps making more metaphors, even in mythical context, one remains in the world of the tangible and physical, and God is neither. Thomas comes back to the tree and the wound, not God himself, even though he tries to associate them with God. The tree and the hole or wound become merely two more metaphors, even though they are deep and universal ones. They appear to be universal, because they explode the basis of accepted knowledge altogether. They go back to the original fork in existence. They express equally deep and universal suffering, and the sum total is that God has to be articulated because without that our existence is both unbearable and unintelligible. But the metaphors still do not render God himself.

It is said that Thomas was influenced by Ted Hughes's *Crow* in writing these poems. Whether this is so or not, Thomas fairly soon leaves the mode behind. Instead he starts to move away from the tangible. This culminates in *Frequencies*, where God as absent, and as always a step ahead and out of sight, comes the topic, and the writing becomes not a description of God but a search for God. This itself is something the poet concedes, or cries, or ironically confesses. Something of this begins in *Laboratories of the Spirit* too, although in that book the distinctive poems use the more formal tradition of prayer, and devotional approach, as a mode of expression on which the poems enter. But it seems that in postulating this most unknowable, now non-mythical God, the poet runs up against a difficulty in language itself.

It is a question of how the contrived writing is to come, what is left to be said when the startling metaphors can no longer be the statement. The latter becomes one of what sort of language can describe absence itself, the God who is not physically manageable, yet still exists or at least possibly may do so. Thomas is explicit on the need for this matter of the language to be faced. In 'The

Absence' (*Frequencies*) he remarks that "I modernize the anachronism of my language" while in 'Cancellation' (*Poetry Wales* Spring 1979, hitherto uncollected) the position is confronted more fully:

> Facility
> of the pen with old
> words, images from a time
> that was past had continually
> to be checked. The natural
> world was his temptation,
> providing the adjectives
> that discredit.

The result is that in this period Thomas enters on a new flow or current of language. He has to recognize the fragmented nature of modern discourse, the human speech that can no longer name reliable entities and events, and instead is simply the minimal, often desperate language by which we keep in touch with each other at all. The pain continues. There are elisions, incomplete sequences of thought or feeling, apparent doubts, cancellings, and half-expressions leading to spontaneous connections. The reader is drawn in to fill the form out, or at least partake in it even if incompleteness is still the outcome, so that a dialogue, irritated argument, or surprising connection has occurred. The existence of morse-code daily discourse is, tacitly, acknowledged. This is not to say that all of Thomas's poems are now fragmented. Rather, several modes of discourse are entered or temporarily take him over.

At times this will seem to have little to do with God. Sometimes a staccato abruptness comes when the pronoun is omitted:

> Stopped the car, asked a man the way,
> To some place; he rested on it
> Smiling....
>
> ('That Day')

Sometimes a wearied reflection is entered upon nonetheless apparently spontaneously:

> Oh, I know it: the long story,
> The ecstasies, the mutilations;
> Crazed, pitiable creatures
> Imagining themselves a Napoleon,

A Jesus; letting their hair grow,
Shaving it off
                          ('This One')

Other poems go in for all kinds of general reflection:

Life, too, fights against itself.
The mother-in-law has her revenge...
                          ('The In-Law')

It is as though, along with the mythic figuring and refiguring of
God, there now has to be engagement with almost any aspect of the
past or present world. History, galactic science and the urban scene
are all entered. This would appear to be not simply to approach the
final elucidation by virtue of first having gathered all the 'evidence'.
It is also as though to clear the ground and trappings of all earthly
existence out of the way, so that the absent God can be encountered
in whatever language remains.

This takes many forms in this period. In a number of poems the
poet, like Yeats, does subject his multifarious thoughts to a unity, or
perhaps finds they shape themselves that way. This is of some
import in seeing how Thomas and language mutually engage. Here
is an entire poem to illustrate it:

Mostly it was wars
With their justification
Of the surrender of values
For which they fought. Between
Them they laid their plans
For the next, exempted
From compact by the machine's
Exigencies. Silence
Was out of date; wisdom consisted
In a revision of the strict code
Of the spirit. To keep moving
Was best; to bring the arrival
Nearer departure; to synchronize
The applause, as the public images
Stepped on or off the stationary
Aircraft. The labour of the years
Was over; the children were heirs
To an instant existence. They fed the machine

Their questions, knowing the answers
Already, unable to apply them.
                              ('Digest')

This is profoundly historical. It summarizes an era still with us as though it was past, just as it sees a past prior to that too, in that what brought on this present time is that "the labour of the years/Was over". It is also abstract and general, with only a few palpable things; and its summary terseness is ironic, as much as to say that so much effort and pain was scarcely worthwhile if it can all be captured in a few brief phrases. Major parts of metaphysical reality, "silence" and "existence", are given the epithets of a two-dimensional and shallow view of time: "out of date" and "instant"; and the shift into something like a language of real metaphysics of time ("to keep loving/Was best; to bring the arrival/Nearer departure") turns out to be just as hollow in its embodiment in daily life. For only images, not people, step on and off the aircraft which, in a poem moved through and through with time, nevertheless stand still themselves. The conclusion alludes to an activity which is self-defeating.

Yet along with this, we are left with the poem's shaping feature, the regular weighting of the phrases. Each terse observation seems of the same import as all the others, and only once or twice is a qualification included. This feature of Thomas's writing has not appeared before this period. Also in this particular poem, the mode is that of synechdoche; that is to say, each phrase seems to stand in very briefly for a whole wider package of activities, trends and tendencies, and this too is a common mode with Thomas in this period. But the way the phrases follow each other as in a list, so that any organic form is only inserted by the reader, seems paramount. Indeed the poem could be started in the middle, read to the end, then round from the beginning to the same middle point, with not much difference of effect.

This new tendency to render material as lists, perhaps to hear or feel it so in the first place, seems after all natural in a poet who is so relentless in his perceptions, tightly controlling them all and letting none dominate the others. It is also ironic. It is as though Thomas feels, for a time, that nothing is worth more than anything else, and that all is level. The poem 'Remedies' is very similar, ending not with a summary flowering figure but one more reduction: "Fortunes

were made/On the ability to disappoint". Even the very beautiful
and quite different poem 'Nocturne by Ben Shahn', an exchange
somewhat after the manner of Wallace Stevens, has every speech a
line in length, equally weighted. In two poems, 'Farming Peter' in
Laboratories of the Spirit and the title poem 'H'm' itself, there is no
punctuation at all, and the poems are thus simply lists of words.
They make phrases, but each is joined to the next by the ordinary
conjunction, 'and' or 'but'. In each, the utterly levelled movement
renders the evoked people helpless. 'Taste', a list of personal
responses to poets of the English tradition, makes clear distinctions
of value between poet and poet, but the levelling structure still seems
to take judgement itself back to a knowing mockery of the poet who
commits himself to such aphoristic evaluations. Possibly most interesting is 'The Calling'. In this poem every sentence except the first
is in the imperative mood, an injunction. The ironic turns to the
tragic, in that the strong metaphors of the Thomas hallmark ("the
crumpled ticket of your prayers") bring a quality of worth even to
the bleakest observations of the parish people the reader is enjoined
to visit. But the elaborated picture at the end is sobering:

> Learn the thinness
> of the window that is
> between you and life, and how
> the mind cuts itself if it goes through.

Because these poems, after the mythic ones, seem to dominate
much of this period, other poems which are more complex seem to
come up against difficulty, and to end by letting the difficulty rest
and remain. They are thus both more positive and sadder. Here is
'Petition':

> And I standing in the shade
> Have see it a thousand times
> Happen: first a theft, then murder;
> Rape; the rueful acts
> Of the blind hand. I have said
> New prayers, or said the old
> In a new way. Seeking the poem
> In the pain, I have learned
> Silence is best, paying for it
> With my conscience. I am eyes
> Merely, witnessing virtue's

Defeat; seeing the young born
Fair, knowing the cancer
Awaits them. One thing I have asked
Of the disposer of the issues
Of life: that truth should defer
To beauty. It was not granted.

Broadly this much-quoted poem demonstrates a latent residue of the
role of priest. He is still staring, still the observer ("I am
eyes/Merely"), yet an appointed observer, although no one phrase
states this nor is it formally underwritten. Rather, a certain assump-
tion of stance conveys this feeling. But how very differently "silence
is best" weighs down this poem's centre, in contrast to the way
"silence/Was out of date" merely followed in place in 'Digest', considered earlier. The language in 'Petition' suggests the poet is feeling
the consequence at the moment of writing it. Each sadly felt observation comes out of the previous one rather than just lying down
after it. In poems like these in these three books it is as though the
poet tries to push out, by a foray, into some part of life that will
bring hope, a possibility of direction, to escape the deadness that
listed language puts into or finds in everything daily around us and
its only possible articulation.

We have said then that this period's poems are about God. Yet
the poet so far has only been able to postulate a mythic and objec-
tionable God, and then to enter the secular godless language of our
time. He becomes prey to a wintry reductionism as to past history
and the present world; and even when a sadder, less ironic feeling
is presented the end is tragic and dark. Is there any way that God
can be found through twentieth century language, the language the
poet cannot avoid adopting? It is a very complex matter, and there
is no way to deal with it but to go through the abstract kind of questioning the topic demands.

For example, some modern theologians, linking arms with the
new wave of psychoanalysts and linguists, have newly articulated the
idea of God's Word. The Word is not now seen by them as either
definitive sacred books, nor a set of imposed theological laws. Rather
language itself is God's Word, imprinted with a prior pattern to
which we are subject. As Heidegger put it, we do not speak language, language speaks us. But how can a poet articulate God if this
is so? Does the poet let God's language flow through him in some
way, or open himself or herself passively to that? The results we

have considered, not in any way failing as poetry, do not seem to
articulate God. Is there some other way?

This brings us particularly to *Laboratories of the Spirit*. In a
number of poems in this book there is prayer. Prayer of course is an
address to God rather than from God, yet the traditional Christian
idea that one can only pray receptively, suggests that prayer too
might be an articulation of God's own language. To pray receptively
would seem to allow the receiver of the prayer to be the source of
what the prayer is about. In these poems prayer occurs, or is
approached, in more than one way. The poems 'Emerging', 'The
Flower', 'The Combat', 'Alive' and 'Pardon' are all addresses to
God, although not all name him, and they move between devotion,
meditation and rather sad cry. 'The Combat' and 'Pardon' begin
prayerfully, but by the end have ceased to pray altogether. 'The
Prayer' and 'The Moon in Lleyn' are about prayer but from the outside. The speaker in the poem is not praying, at least not during the
poem's time. 'Sea-watching' and 'Ivan Karamazov' allude to prayer,
while 'Suddenly' and 'Dialogue' might perhaps be regarded as aris-
ing from prayer which is not itself present. In all these poems the
poet appears to be striving for articulation of God through this
mode of prayer, just as he attempted the same thing in the mythic
poems but by another method. In both, a firm shape from a traditional mode (religious myth; prayer) is used as a quasi-substitute for
the God who cannot be found by art. Art has form by its nature,
but this God is formless.

'Emerging' is the most direct form of prayer, and begins the
book:

> Not as in the old days I pray,
> God. My life is not what it was.
> Yours, too, accepts the presence of
> the machine? Once I would have asked
> healing. I go now to be doctored,
> to drink sinlessly of the blood
> of my brother, to lend my flesh
> as manuscript of the great poem
> of the scalpel.

The poet begins to pray, but from a recognition that prayer itself
has changed. It is the machine, contemporary technology, that has
made the difference, for God is asked whether that is present for

him too. Furthermore the new technology is biological as well as
mechanical and electronic. Yet, after going on to resort to prayer's
most naked cry a few lines later – "Hear my prayer, Lord, hear my
prayer" – it is as though nothing further can be said in this way:

> It begins to appear
> this is not what prayer is about.
> It is the annihilation of difference,
> the consciousness of myself in you,
> of you in me...

and the poet concludes in a new position altogether, one that
appears to put aside, after all, any dependence on either Eden or the
tree where the wounded body hangs.

> I begin to recognise
> you anew, God of form and number.
> There are questions we are the solution
> to, others whose echoes we must expand
> to contain. Circular as our way
> is, it leads not back to that snake-haunted
> garden, but onward to the tall city
> of glass that is the laboratory of the spirit.

This poem contains much that is significant. The phrase realiz-
ing that "this is not what prayer is about", does not sound prayerful,
or an address to God, at all. It is like any thought one might have
about anything. Yet at the same time the "annihilation of difference"
must allow the meditation to be thought of as directly from God, as
though God, in some sense at least, in part originated it. This turning inside-out of prayer is parallelled in the rest of the poem.
Self-knowledge becomes not a reflection of the self, but a trans-
parency of self to self, an imbuing of the self with consciousness.
Thomas's recurrent symbol of the mirror for self-knowledge, as
though both oneself and the mirror are tangible things, gives way to
a perception unresolvable and metaphysical; "There are questions
we are the solution to". The symbol of that is not now mirror but
glass; what we see *through*; and it is as though this is found only in
the technological world which can offer the "tall city/of glass" which
itself can be seen through, and so perhaps understood. If God is to
be encountered it will be through the high-rise blocks of Dallas and

Singapore if there is to be a palpable medium at all. Yet "questions...whose echoes we must expand/to contain" suggest it may not
even be palpable.

But that stage is not reached yet, and the remaining poems of
prayer in this book either gather round a strong physical analogue,
or falter and cease to be prayers. 'The Flower' and 'Sea-watching'
both present a scene or thing which stand in for God or some act
of God. They are ambivalent however, for they both parallel the
divine presence but also, by being so vividly present, stop the
approach to the absent formless God himself. 'Alive' is more
straightforwardly devotional, a true poem of praise in a line that
descends from George Herbert. It suggests that the real earth is an
emanation from God rather than merely comparable to him. In 'The
Flower', it is almost as though the poet begins by feeling an articulation of God directly, but is interrupted by the magnetic effect of
the beautiful world of earth, sea and sky God has put in front of
him. At first "I looked at them/and learned I must withdraw/to possess them". That is to say, again he must not play with enjoyable
metaphor for its own sake if God is to be attained; and as a result
the poet "dwelt/in a soundless darkness/in the shadow/of your
regard". To be without sound or light is nearly to be without the
palpable altogether: yet what is beautiful irrepressibly returns. "The
soul/grew in me, filling me/with its fragrance". The poet does not
resist this interruption, and goes back finally to the sort of comparison we have long realized he finds irresistibly congenial:

> Men came
> to me from the four
> winds to hear me speak
> of the unseen flower by which
> I sat, whose roots were not
> in the soil, nor its petals the colour
> of the wide sea; that was
> its own species with its own
> sky over it, shot
> with the rainbow of your coming and going.

It is still a difficulty of language. The magnetic force of the
metaphor of the flower for itself draws away from its efficacy to
serve prayer as a further end. It is a beautiful image and poem; yet,
in others, the poet pushes on and seeks further. In 'The Prayer', the

poet approaches this difficulty explicitly again as he did in 'Emerging', with which the book started. He knows almost at once what is wrong:

> He kneeled down
> dismissing his orisons
> as inappropriate; one by one
> they came to his lips and were swallowed
> but without bile.
> He fell back
> on an old prayer: Teach me to know
> what to pray for.

As in 'Emerging' he falls back on an old prayer, the new being "inappropriate"; and that word carries its own deep irony, being drawn as it is from the inappropriate vocabulary of bureaucracy and public relations technique. Its governing of the archaic "orisons" bleakly underlines the inappropriateness. Again, as so often, he turns to metaphor, holding out his hands now not together as in prayer, but "cupped/as though to receive blood, leaking from life's side". Again the wound, of language this time, appears.

And in 'The Combat', Thomas does battle with both God and language difficulty at once:

> You have no name.
> We have wrestled with you all
> day, and now night approaches....
> For the failure of language
> there is no redress.

One feels a certain humility at this courageous poet's determination, in spite of all, not to be deterred by apparently insurmountable difficulties. He is after all a priest, and his duty requires him to find a way of articulating God if it can possibly be done. He is close to Herbert in these prayer poems. The form of the titles echoes Herbert: 'The Hand', 'The Word', 'The Prayer', 'The Combat', 'The Reception', 'The Problem', 'The Casualty'. They seem nearest to formality, as against those stark one-word titles, often adverbs or pronouns, that Thomas uses so often elsewhere, 'Thus', 'This', 'That', 'So', 'Somewhere', 'Which'. One poem, however, which expresses this determination in face of such barriers, seems to culminate the

prayer poems in *Laboratories of the Spirit* and perhaps the book itself.
   This is 'The Moon in Lleyn', held to be a major poem by many
readers of Thomas, and one in which certainly many of the foregoing themes and tropes are assembled in quick succession:

> The last quarter of the moon
> of Jesus gives way
> to the dark; the serpent
> digests the egg. Here
> on my knees in this stone
> church, that is full only
> of the silent congregation
> of shadows and the sea's
> sound, it is easy to believe
> Yeats was right. Just as though
> choirs had not sung, shells
> have swallowed them; the tide laps
> at the Bible; the bell fetches
> no people to the brittle miracle
> of the bread. The sand is waiting
> for the running back of the grains
> in the wall into its blond
> glass. Religion is over, and
> what will emerge from the body
> of the new moon no one
> can say.
>   But a voice sounds
> in my ear: Why so fast, mortal? These very seas
> are baptized. The parish
> has a saint's name time cannot
> unfrock. In cities that
> have outgrown their promise people
> are becoming pilgrims
> again, if not to this place,
> then to the recreation of it
> in their own spirits. You must remain
> kneeling. Even as this moon
> making its way through the earth's
> cumbersome shadow, prayer, too,
> has its phrases.

Thomas's two long-used symbols of empty church and bread
appear at once, though now differently, and newly quickened.

However, although the priest-poet is in the physical attitude of prayer, he is apparently not at this moment praying but reflecting. At first it may sound pessimistic, but what follows is too clear-sighted, too much a marshalling of evidence, for mere melancholy. As a result, "Yeats was right" sounds positive. R.S. Thomas is being as explicit about the moon's phases and a second coming, if of a different sort, as Yeats was in his own major poems on the same matters. The end of the phases of the moon in Christian context is here no matter of mere human error or stupidity. It is deeply elemental. Music, sea, stone and bread move to their right places along a course in one sense determined, in another sense tapping the universe's deepest energy. "Fetches" is a very exact word, as though it too was a physical action. Consequently when "Yeats was right" is in its turn balanced by a three-word declaration, it too sounds decisive and proud, allowing the facing of a wholly uncertain future with equally confident resonance:

> Religion is over, and
> what will emerge from the body
> on the new moon, no one
> can say.

The paragraph ends there, but it is curiously strong in the light of its theme. It is as though it has cleared the ground for an answer in the same terms of elements and time. The question that begins the second half is yet another three-word phrase, and tersely modern in tone: "why so fast?". Yet it also sounds as though it is heard in a sea-shell itself, so tightly is the poem bound in with the elements and natural objects it evokes. It is the same "sounds" as those of the sea in the first part of the poem. Consequently, even if people do not return to the church itself, the church will stand, the people restoring it in "the recreation of it in their own spirits". Even if the parish's name were to change – St Petersburg to Leningrad, so to speak – the old name is ineradicably lodged. The conclusion is an enjoining of a return to a timeless attitude of prayer which has not yet ceased despite the curvature of wider cosmic movements.

I feel it is a profound and exciting poem which will endure. Despite the difficulties, an earthly position is at least temporarily secured. The metaphoric attitude, so to call it, remains serviceable. Regardless of the new technologies which distract, stone, sea and wider universe do not go away, and to "remain kneeling" is thus tenable, for it can be seen to merge with those wider movements.

Nevertheless the poet's main difficulty, about language, is not resolved by 'The Moon in Lleyn'. It may be that in expectation of the people's real or analogical return he is right to stay by the church, so far as that goes. But, in this and the other prayer poems, he has still not found the language that emanates from and returns to God from humanity through our thin, two-dimensional language of today. Prayer is necessary but is not enough. If a chance remains that such language is to be found he must still look for it. This would not be a language from God through the poet to the people; R.S. Thomas is no evangelist. It would be a language from our modern world but usable in the approach to God. This brings us to the third book of this period, *Frequencies*.

In this book there are a number of poems which grapple with this matter of verbal language. This time it is a matter not just of language but language to God. It is verbal language, of course, that is most pressing to the poet; but in the book, as the title suggests, verbal language is gradually seen to be only one of many approaches to whatever is ultimate and calling upon us or else eluding us. This is designated here as elsewhere as 'God'. But the frequencies on which the poet taps out his message and waits in silence for an answer, include the radio wave and sea wave (and the fishing line), the thought process itself, numbers, and waves of light. And many of the language poems themselves, naturally, are immersed in the wider act of probing which is the book's chief characteristic, and which finds, in the end, that the entity hoped for does not come, and when it is approached, recedes. But verbal language is the mode the poet most stops by to examine for its nature itself, sadly, impatiently and so often ironically in such a way as to ironize the very language it uses.

The opening poem 'The Gap' is like the myth poems of *H'm*, but is directly about language. It is about the naming of God, and it begins with a somewhat effete God reclining on a cloud and watching in alarm as a tower of speech grows toward him. God's name alone is missing:

> One word more and
> it would be on a level
> with him; vocabulary
> would have triumphed.

God's response is to sign his name in the dictionary's blank space, but by letting his own blood. There then appears

> The sign in the space
> on the page, that is in all languages
> and none; that is the grammarian's
> torment and the mystery
> at the cell's core, and the equation
> that will not come out, and is
> the narrowness that we stare
> over into the eternal
> silence that is the repose of God.

We have here the very ancient idea that one cannot name God, whatever mode of knowledge we use; yet we notice that God does sign his name, does presumably exist. But we are still not told what the name is either, and God continues to occupy his silence. On a rather different front of language, there is another notable feature of this poem, and that is its very long last sentence (the one just quoted). Soon after, in 'The Truce', the same feature occurs:

> Such truce as was
> called in the invisible
> warfare between bad and
> worse was where two half-truths
> faced one another over
> the body of an exhausted
> nation, each one waiting for
> the other to be proved wrong.

The short lines prevent us from getting any purchase on the sentence until it is finished, by which time a sort of cluster or swelling of idea and image has been gathered and, for the moment, the endless deferral can seem arrested. 'The Gap' (both poems so named), 'Ivan Karamazov', 'Poste Restante', 'The Chapel', 'The Porch', 'Hesitations', 'Dialectic', 'Gone?' and several others end with these very long sentences; convoluted and extended forms of expression by which at least some saturation of meaning is stored up. The normally linear flow of two-dimensional language circles on itself, and the often abstract and non-figurative language feels thereby enriched, because consciousness itself does too.

This control or restraining of the forward movement of consciousness itself, as though to capture a piece of identity in some shape or other and hold it briefly still, seems an increasing need of Thomas in this period. It, too, is a preparation for the final articulation the poet seeks, although he will continue to use it after his articulation of God (as far as that turns out to be possible) is consummated. In 'Shadows', the attempt at other language is different. The poet gives himself to listening for the language that is needed. The poet closes his eyes, but then finds it is as much the darkness as the light of God that blinds. He therefore turns to the medium that matters:

> And so I listen
> instead and hear the language
> of silence, the sentence
> without an end. Is it I, then,
> who am being addressed? A God's words
> are for their own sake; we hear
> at our peril. Many of us have gone
> mad in the mastering
> of your medium.

This is a curious, ambivalent passage. The madness seems to have the alliteration of an Anglo-Saxon kenning, and so echoes very anciently. The idea that we are addressed by God is equally old. Yet the previous sentence, about "the sentence/without an end" has the ring of modern, indeed contemporary thought about language; the language which is no longer confident in its power to name and so expresses only an incessant yet deferred desire. We enter upon speech, only to find that we are naming nothing. The thing we thought we had named is pushed on into the future ahead of us. We have entered only on an expression of our unconscious; we even find that it is, rather, expressing us.

What then is this 'language search' amounting to in the poet's work at this time? What we gradually find, is that the attempt to articulate God turns out again and again to do that only insofar as God's elusiveness, his receding before the poet, is itself what gets expressed. And the theological question – also sought as to its expression in some poems – is whether that experience of an absence is itself some guarantee that the absence is one that a presence has vacated. This quest and its expression are the consummation and perhaps the nodal-point of Thomas's entire work when we look back at it over the years. This is not to say it is or is not the best (that is a different question surely altogether), nor that there is not much more to come. Poem after poem in *Frequencies* is marked with a brief passage about God's absence, God not there where he could have been, or was a little while before, or who might come if we are patient, or who has left a small sign of his presence but one which gives no further assurance he will ever be apprehended again. After and along with poems on the dead machine, biochemistry, historical disaster, myths of evil and the poet's own soul-searching, it is as though at last God's actual absence must itself be alluded to, without inserting anything else which might distract or substitute:

the emptiness that was where God
should have been
    ('Perhaps')

               We never catch
him at work, but can only say,
coming suddenly upon an amendment,
that here he has been.
    ('Adjustments')

He is a religious man.
How often I have heard him say,
looking around him with his worried eyes
at the emptiness: There must be something.
    ('The Possession')

           Surely for one
with patience he will happen by
once in a while
    ('Emerging')

                ...waited
for the figure that cast it
to come into view for us to
identify it, and it
didn't and we are still waiting.
    ('The Film of God')

             such a fast
God, always before us and
leaving as we arrive.
    ('Pilgrimages')

And from 'The Absence', which seems to be the definitive poem on
the whole matter:

> What recourse have I
> other than the emptiness without him of my whole
> being, a vacuum he may not abhor?

All these examples are found toward the end of *Frequencies*. Here
in at last confronting the necessity of the approach of this kind,
Thomas is adopting the traditional and indeed ancient attitude of
the mediaeval mystics. The anonymous author of the fourteenth
century tract *The Cloud of Unknowing* suggests that giving attention
to anything at all, even good things, perhaps even God's "qualities",
is a distraction from encounter with God. Rather, Thomas turns to
a more complex articulation of the questions that need, not to be
answered, but to be expressed, allowing only the minimum of physical, that is figurative reference:

> To learn to distrust the distrust
> of feeling – this then was the next step
> for the seeker? To suffer himself to be persuaded
> of intentions in being other than the crossing
> of a receding boundary which did not exist?
> To yield to an unfelt pressure that, irresistible
> in itself, had the character of everything
> but coercion? To believe, looking up
> into invisible eyes shielded against love's
> glare, in the ubiquity of a vast concern?
>
> ('Perhaps')

The passage is very illustrative of the tenor of *Frequencies*. It
avoids easy comparisons, yet risks being accused of another easy
way; namely, that of simply playing words and notions round each
other so as to produce a language structure complete grammatically,
but referring to nothing. But in fact, the questions in this passage
are not merely balanced equations that work out to zero. The language feels intentional, even anxious. The way that successive parts
of each sentence seem to cancel out what went before, leaves the
verb still hanging, "suffer", "yield", "believe", as though wondering
what caused those experiences in the first place. You cannot just
suffer, yield or believe in isolation. You have to suffer something,
yield to something, and believe or believe in something. The self-

cancelling things, the receding boundary which however did not exist, the pressure already unfelt which was irresistible yet did not coerce, and so on, are not quite mere self-contradiction. Nor however do they appear to be simply psychological, unless we beg the question and assume that in the first place. What Thomas really is articulating is, of course, for every reader to decide separately; but he is as close as anyone could be, it seems, to expressing 'absence' as itself an entity, as implying of necessity a presence before, after or beside, by which the resulting absence could have pressure, and seem to hint at something not itself, and so not be mere flat emptiness. There is therefore only absence in terms of the limited human apprehension that knows no way of making it present, or finding the language that will call it up.

Thomas looks for this absent God everywhere. Surprisingly perhaps, one place to search is back in Wales. This is the case in 'Llananno', 'That Day' and 'The Signpost'. The matter of Wales is no longer overtly political at all, and in fact a new use of the country has already been set out in one or two earlier poems in *Frequencies*, notably 'The Small Country'. In the three poems just cited however, the sense of a receding presence is caught obliquely in that the poet sees the landscape, or something in it, in the course of a car journey. Again, then, what is sought does not remain quite still. In these poems the poet is not returning to a point at which to stay, for he only "calls" at the small church by the river at Llananno, and as for Casgob (in 'The Signpost'), "I never went/there". The poems like so many in this period are intriguing in their ambivalence. In one way they contrast the mystic's approach to God, for they tie him so inescapably to the material; they relentlessly invoke the very language that, it seemed, must be put aside if the different language for the absent God is to be heard. They arouse "the temptation of the natural world" again; they invoke "the adjectives that discredit". Yet, in a different way, these places seem to call up the experience of the eternal as much as anything else. In the church at Llananno the poet finds he is "face to face/with no intermediary/between me and God", while his very failure to follow the signpost to Casgob has a spiritual significance:

> Time
> is a main road, eternity
> the turning that we don't take.

Strangely, there is a certain ease, and even a relief, in these poems. But again it turns out to be only temporary. At the surface level, one might put it that the poet is for a brief moment letting himself believe in a luxury; namely, that the natural landscape, poetry and old church are in some simple way a direct emanation of God. The God who eludes when all palpable things, even the senses themselves, are left behind, can suddenly be experienced in what is immediate and natural. Clearly this contrasts the position as it has seemed to be expressed in the poems of this period considered so far, which was that removal of what is physical and palpable is entailed if God is to be confronted. What Thomas seems to be acknowledging here, however, is that if God does indeed exist and, in some sense, created the physical world, then that fact may well be experienced from time to time in the physical world. The distinction is however that the fact is experienced, not God himself. Again therefore Thomas finds that this expression, very human and genuine and indeed of theological value as far as it goes, does not have a timeless dimension that lasts, and its place is limited.

Another mode of approach to the godhead lies through technology and pure science. Like every modern poet, Thomas has to grapple with a new science which necessitates an entirely new picture of matter-energy, and of the cosmos. In Thomas's case the special difference is that it modifies and in the end controls his understanding of God and his approach to God. Thomas adduces everything from technology –

> Sound, too? The recorder
> that picks up everything picked
> up nothing but the natural
> background. What language
> does the god speak?
>   ('The Film of God')

– through biochemistry –

> Oh, I know it and don't
> care. I know there is nothing in me
> but cells and chromosomes
> waiting to beget chromosomes
> and cells...
>   ('Bravo!')

– through the great scientists –

> I think he sits at that strange table
> of Eddington's, that is not a table
> at all, but nodes and molecules
> pushing against molecules
> and nodes; and he writes there
> in invisible handwriting the instructions
> the genes follow.
>
> ('At It')

– to cosmology:

> What they are saying is
> that there is life there too;
> that the universe is the size it is
> to enable us to catch up.
>
> They have gone on from the human;
> that shining is a reflection
> of their intelligence. Godhead
> is the colonization by mind
>
> of untenanted space. It is its own
> light, a statement beyond language
> of conceptual truth. Every night
> is a rinsing myself of the darkness
>
> that is in my veins. I let the stars inject me
> with fire, silent as it is far,
> but certain in its cauterising
> of my despair. I am a slow
>
> traveller, but there is more than time
> to arrive. Resting in the intervals
> of my breathing, I pick up the signals
> relayed to me from a periphery I comprehend.
>
> ('Night Sky')

"There is more than time/to arrive" has a double meaning, characteristically muted and easily overlooked. All these examples are from *Frequencies*. Thomas is here clearly in line with late-twentieth century post-positivistic science, which can no longer easily postulate

either the detached observer, nor dead and meaningless matter as
the basis of all that is observed. Sometimes God inheres, sometimes
is distant, sometimes nowhere at all; but in each case the poet seems
to feel we inhabit a strange, yet curiously known galactic cosmos and
space. As a result, Thomas's moods and attitudes shift from place
to place and from moment to moment. Sometimes it is calm:

> So truth must appear
> to the thinker; so, at a stage
> of the experiment, the answer
> must quietly emerge...
>   ('Suddenly')

Elsewhere it is more awestruck:

> So in the huge night,
> awakening, I have re-interpreted
> the stars' signals and seen the reflection
> in an eternal mirror of the mystery
> terrifying enough to be named Love.
>   ('Scenes')

The poet enters the vocabulary and language of our scientific apprehension, and lets them play over his responses to which he becomes
attached. It is as though, in surrendering to a new science's way of
seeing things, R.S. Thomas has experienced a certain sense of won-
derment now gone calm, such that human calamity and ignominy
may be seen in more serene perspective. The new science is no longer
a series of results of experiments; it has projected a cosmos larger
than itself, larger than it expected. And this entails a response which
may be called 'religious' in a broad sense acceptable to anyone. In a
narrower sense of religious, the possibility of articulating God is pursued into all these corners, vast spaces, phenomena seen through
microscope or radiotelescope only, and places of darkness or light.

Expression of the inexpressible, catching of detail about the
absent God who yet must have been there, is also attempted in
abstraction itself. The landscape of the small country is found mysteriously receding, the cosmos itself is peered into as though space
itself defines the greatest absence of all; yet further, to put thought
conceptually is also to take us out of the everyday on track of, perhaps, the infinite. There is then this third stage of language, in effect

a third layer of language wholly conceptual which intervenes from
time to time. R.S. Thomas touches on this wordless language by
means of words:

> There is a language
> beyond speech we are given to learn
> by a suspension of the categories
> of the present.
>
> ('Scenes')

> And
> there is the indefinable point,
> the incarnation of a concept,
> the moment at which a little
> becomes a lot.
>
> ('Abercuawg')

The long passage of this kind from the end of 'Perhaps' was cited
earlier. In less interrogative mood something like the same apprehension is reached in 'Dialectic':

> If there were words once
> they could not understand, I will show
> them now space that is bounded
> but without end, time that is where
> they were or will be; the eternity
> that is here for me and for them
> there; the truth that with much labour
> is born with them and is to be
> sloughed off like some afterbirth of the spirit.

If absence, as said earlier, is not mere flat emptiness, but a state
whose very nature must somehow hint at meaningfulness, somehow
suggest that in its absentness is a sort of residue of what is away, then
this too may be got at by words to some degree. The state of mind
or spirit which experiences this not pointless absence, will itself give
rise to rhythm, qualitative strings of expressions however tenuous, a
sort of verbal embodiment of the very nature of justified yearning or
spiritual intuition itself. That humans may long for something to be
in the cosmic or universal void after all, and for that desire not to
seem merely psychological restlessness or fantasizing alone, something in language itself is necessary. It is necessary that expressions

using the most longlived, universal, deeply sensed categories we have
– time, space, thought, love, other, being, nothing, all – should seem
to hold in themselves something yet further still, something just
beyond reach of our words, or any words, which however still feel
meaningful and which, in effect, posit an object of our deepest and
most final aspirations. If any poetry can seem to achieve this, to pull
us forward in ways which *ex hypothesi* cannot be expressed, then one
might put it that the religious option is still open even in a world that
does not acknowledge any direct divine manifestation of a traditional
sort. That at least is what I take it Thomas is acting on, in employ-
ing poetry's special power of getting the most resonance out of
conceptions used more categorically outside of poetry, to convey our
deepest experiences in more organized fashion.

Many poems, then, in *Frequencies* particularly, circle this central
notion of God's absence. Not all engage with it directly. But this,
already a demanding ambition for any poet, must have been particularly so for one whose everyday apprehension of the world is so
couched in one bodily mode so strongly; namely, the act of seeing.
Seeing, even staring, has never been far from Thomas's way of
understanding the world. In 'The Observer' in *Not That He Brought
Flowers*, in 'Petition' which we cited earlier, and in those very earliest poems in *Song at the Year's Turning* when the young priest stood
and stared at the peasant working in a nearby field, this channel or
path to reality has been robustly employed, and powerfully assumed
as to what it will yield in obvious returns from everyday life. In these
more recent poems in *Frequencies* the poet seems to have deliberately
put this powerful tool aside, and the phrase "denial of the flesh"
takes on a new, if quite unexpected meaning. Does this putting aside
of seeing find any expression itself, and is it itself used in any way
as analogue of the quest for the invisible? I think it does and is,
although only in one poem does it reach a full, total expression.
Elsewhere it is touched on briefly, as though the poet knows well
that this seeing must be by passed if he is to inhabit a spiritual
domain where God, either present or absent, is no object for the
naked eye. In 'Suddenly', the poem makes the distinction clearly
enough: "I looked/at him not with the eye/only, but with the
whole/of my being, overflowing with/him as a chalice would/with the
sea". That is certainly attractive, but is a figure only; it does not tell
us too much about the distinction itself. In two poems Thomas re-
employs his now familiar symbol of the mirror. In these however the

mirror no longer means self-knowledge only. It is now something not to see in, but to see past. In 'Ffynon Fair (St Mary's Well)' the poet stares down, but qualifies. "Ignoring my image, I peer down/to the quiet roots of it, where/the coins lie". This poem along with 'Groping' suggests perhaps a renewed influence of Wordsworth at this stage, except that the riches at the bottom of the well are spiritual currency rather specifically. In 'Pre-Cambrian' the new use of the mirror is a little more elaborate:

> I am charmed here
> by the serenity of the reflections
> in the sea's mirror. It is a window
> as well. What I need
> now is a faith to enable me to out-stare
> the grinning faces of the inmates of its asylum,
> the failed experiments God put away.

In both these poems, the second especially, something is added; what 'seeing' can achieve is complex, yet finally limited, and yet again it is through perceptive seeing itself that this result is discovered. In one most memorable and remarkable poem, however, the matter reaches a consummation. This poem is 'Sea-watching', and it is found toward the end of *Laboratories of the Spirit*. In fact it is the last but one poem in that book, as though to clear the ground finally for the rarified and metaphysical straining forward, without benefit of eyesight so to speak, which *Frequencies* embodies.

The poem 'Sea-watching' is haunted by the expanse of sea at which it stares, and its own unusual case of physical watching, of which this poet has had so many years experience. By it, seeing's limits can be found just through the constant examination and re-examination of seeing itself. The poem is based on the practice among ornithologists of focusing their field-glasses on a single spot, motionlessly, for a very long period. This is done in the hope that a bird of rare species, known to inhabit such spots, will alight there. The poem is so compelling, in that in it the poet comes to know physical seeing's own end, and in the same event finds at last a true analogue for his spiritual search:

> Grey waters, vast
> as an area of prayer
> that one enters. Daily

```
            over a period of years
      I have let the eye rest on them.
      Was I waiting for something?
                                    Nothing
      but that continuous waving
            that is without meaning
      occurred.
            Ah, but a rare bird is
      rare. It is when one is not looking,
      at times one is not there
                              that it comes.
      You must wear your eyes out,
      as others their knees.
            I became the hermit
      of the rocks, habited with the wind
      and the mist. There were days,
      so beautiful the emptiness
      it might have filled,
                              its absence
      was as its presence; not to be told
      any more, so single my mind
      after its long fast,
                  my watching from praying.
```

We seem to see and feel the ocean, all the time. The poem is right on the border between optical eyesight and spiritual perception. This border is expressed by the similar edge of the land with its many features, and the unchanging sea, the latter so level that the very act of seeing, itself seems to dissolve, and only "that continuous waving/that is without meaning" is left. As a result, the poet is set free from eyesight, can transfer into the different mode of perception which is spiritual. The poem itself makes this very convincing, for it starts with the poet already watching, as it were before the poem begins and going on after it is over, an undifferentiated act into which meaning will only be brought if the hoped-for bird arrives, which it does not. The uneven and broken lines, and the interspersed ruminations and deep reflections, suggest that the poem was haunted in its writing by the rhythm of the gently moving waves and breaking crests, which were constantly before the poet's eyes during his long vigils. Instead of the bird itself, the focus eventually turns on to an expression of wistfulness, almost a sigh, in the poem's central line: "Ah, but a rare bird is/rare".

This line is itself very rare in Thomas. Only two or three times in his entire work is there such a wistful ejaculation, and never is an adjective so deliberately repeated. By the delicate enjambment of the second "rare", the repetition is not static, not without addition, so that it is as though, instead of the bird flying down, a unique spiritual perception is felt. As a result, the line that follows has a second, profound meaning. In the practice of bird-watching it is simply that, frustratingly, the bird (presumably) comes when you are not looking; but at the spiritual level Thomas has opened the way to his searches into absence itself. In effect, it is not by chance, but by the divine nature, that God will come "when one is not looking"; that is to say, when physical eyesight is put aside as not the fitting mode of approach. So another boundary is reached too, and the fact that "its absence/was as its presence" is "not to be told/any more"; not, at least, by means of the physical and metaphorical analogues of the traditional poet and Thomas's own usually favoured mode.

The limit of seeing, the energy it takes and the fatigue it brings, is expressed therefore in that "you must wear your eyes out", go further than seeing itself. This brings in the poem's continued comparison with prayer, in which act one now remembers the eyes are traditionally shut; the theme of the traditional Christian injunction "watch and pray" is echoed, and is where the poem ends. Physical seeing can be taken no further, and when the bodily eyes are worn out another form of seeing must flow into the vacuum that is left.

Again it must be, then, after all the search, language, silence and fatigue, that absence itself is what the modern secularized apprehension of God entails. Somehow the very absence itself is affirmation of, not God's presence, but God's existence. This is no new idea. The Hebrew poet who cried out "How long, Lord? will thou hide thyself for ever?" (Psalms lxxxix 46), and the mediaeval *deus absconditus*, the God who has withdrawn himself, both expressed it. But Thomas has felt it in the context of a twentieth century cosmos with apparently no outside, a microscopically viewed world we cannot fathom, and a language which somehow stutters and refuses to speak. God's absence can be seen as not just that: a blank, a nothing. The French philosopher Bergson (also adduced by Thomas in this period) has termed 'nothing' as always, for human apprehension anyway, a space where 'something' has to have been. We can never conceive 'nothing' without the outline of a shimmering shape which suggests what has been removed. As

Thomas puts it in 'Abercuawg', "An absence is how we become surer/of what we want". The poem 'The Absence', almost at the end of *Frequencies*, is the most succinct statement of the matter:

> It is this great absence
> that is like a presence, that compels
> me to address it without hope
> of a reply. It is a room I enter
>
> from which someone has just
> gone, the vestibule for the arrival
> of one who has not yet come.
> I modernise the anachronism
>
> of my language, but he is no more here
> than before. Genes and molecules
> have no more power to call
> him up than the incense of the Hebrews
>
> at their altars. My equations fail
> as my words do. What recourse have I
> other than the emptiness without him of my whole
> being, a vacuum he may not abhor?

We can finish this discussion of Thomas's theological or mystical period by returning to that other component of his poetry which has never been long absent; his metaphors. Perhaps surprisingly, they do not diminish in force, nor much in number in this period, not even in *Frequencies*. Of Henry James:

> After the curtains deliberately
> kept drawn, his phrases were servants moving
> silently about the great house of his prose
> letting in sunlight into the empty rooms.
>   ('Henry James')

Of profound questions:

> We pass our hands
> over their surface like blind
> men, feeling for the mechanism
> that will swing them aside.
>   ('The Answer')

Of the familiar empty church:

> They laid this stone trap
> for him, enticing him with candles,
> as though he would come like some huge moth
> out of the darkness to beat there
> ('The Empty Church')

All three of these are from *Frequencies*. Again we notice, particularly in the third case, the way the metaphor is itself a recognition, that the way to the uncharacterizable God is blocked if we rely on the senses for that approach. The answer could lie in the nature of this wider universe in which the approach has to be made. Our universe is manifestly physical, but seems to have no centre or main point of reference, no encountered God and not even a clear base, at the subatomic level, for the physical material that makes it. In it, furthermore, as a physical fact, light is the exception and darkness the rule. And in such a universe, there is no need to grasp the immediately physical so that it sticks, is unforgettable, cannot be taken away. This seems to be the force of the robust metaphors. They are forced into palpable presence by the 'untenanted' absence behind them. They are small handles, objects to grasp for reassurance in what is otherwise apparently a void. In case this sounds merely fanciful we can point to the many occasions when the metaphor concerns some matter otherwise bleak or unpleasant. It is as though, whatever the matter at hand, metaphorizing it can somehow endow it with a worthwhile aspect even when no new material is added. In the traditional terms of Aristotle or Sidney, it delights. Thomas's earlier poetry was able to make metaphor coterminous with poem time after time, because he selected a limited universe as source material. Leaving this small parish behind, he does not give up this sort of metaphor as well; but it turns out that the need it satisfies, or the pleasure it gives, serves his wider purpose. Metaphor, then, is still part of Thomas's gradually explicit approach to this receding, absent God. He first leaves, but then, seemingly, also returns to the physical world for something to go with him in his approach to that phenomenon of absence. For the metaphors have now widened their base from the local landscape the poet inhabits. They include more and more the machine, the virus, oxygen (of the spirit), money, the wheel, mathematical equation, the abyss, the chalice, the car, cities, technological and biochemical components, the TV aerial, and references to various periods of history. The absent God is absent from a great deal, making his dimensions the more universal.

Thomas's feeling for eternity as that which can be grasped only in the moment between anticipation and arrival, is most fully expressed in an experience whose parts seem in most palpable metaphor to surround the absence, unnamed here, yet which was grasped only because it was not looked for:

> I have seen the sun break through
> to illuminate a small field
> for a while, and gone my way
> and forgotten it. But that was the pearl
> of great price, the one field that had
> the treasure in it. I realize now
> that I must give all that I have
> to possess it. Life is not hurrying
>
> on to a receding future, nor hankering after
> an imagined past. It is the turning
> aside like Moses to the miracle
> of the lit bush, to a brightness
> that seemed as transitory as your youth
> once, but is the eternity that awaits you.
>   ('The Bright Field')

The occasion of the spiritual vision in this manner is unique and not repeated, and can never be attained once and for all. For this reason the poet comes back and back to metaphor, as well as to his other tropes, his double-entendres, ironies, and people. And in fact the conclusion seems to be that Thomas never imagined that it could be otherwise. As has been apparent all along, he was articulating that absence and his response to it, not explaining it. To apprehend this absence is "to give all that I have", not in some sense of denying or returning material goods or comforts, but in a recognition that emanations of this absence are unpredictable and ubiquitous. When the momentary experience has occurred, the seeker has not finally laid hold of the elusive quarry; he has simply had one more experience of the way it happens in the world. The beauty and pain lie in the fact that the experience is only found in the physical world from which the poetic and figural are drawn. It is as though the poet had known this all the time:

As I had always known
he would come, unannounced,
remarkable merely for the absence
of clamour. So truth must appear
to the thinker; at a stage
of the experiment, the answer
must quietly emerge. I looked
at him, not with the eye,
only, but with the whole,
of my being, overflowing with
him as a chalice would
with the sea. Yet was he
no more there than before,
his area occupied
by the unhaloed presences...

('Suddenly')

IV. Paintings and Other Perspectives

(*Between Here and Now* 1981, new poems in *Later Poems* 1983,
Ingrowing Thoughts 1985)

As surely as *H'm* started the third period of R.S. Thomas's poetic
production, so surely did *Frequencies* end it. Opinion might differ as
to exactly when the search for an articulation of God, for the time
being at least, is consummated. Perhaps it is at the end of the final
poem, where by referring to his quest in the past tense ("Was the
pilgrimage/I made to come to my own/self...?"), the poet seems to
state that it is done. Or else it may be at the end of the poem 'The
Absence', which we cited in full near the end of the last chapter.
Whichever it is, the probing, longing, emerging, shadow-watching
and the rest are finished, or at least suspended before being taken
up again later from the standpoint of a position now achieved. What
is remarkable, is how very differently the next period is begun, and
how firmly the poet seems to suggest that something new is to be
undertaken.

The first thirty-three poems of the next book, *Between Here and
Now*, are a self-contained set, separately called 'Impressions', and
each one is a response to one of thirty-three French Impressionist
paintings which hang in the Louvre in Paris. The paintings are
reproduced in monochrome opposite each poem. Four years later
Thomas gave us a second such set of poems, this time constituting
a whole, if short, collection, *Ingrowing Thoughts*, which contained
twenty-one poems. Again a series of paintings is reproduced in
monochrome opposite the poems. In this later collection, however,
the paintings are all drawn from the twentieth century high period
of modern art; that is to say, surrealism, Cubism and other post-
expressionist modes. In between these two sets of poems about
paintings Thomas also published many new poems of what, in
shorthand, one can call the more ordinary kind. Some thirty more
poems make up the rest of the first book *Between Here and Now*; and
in the *Later Poems 1972-82*, although it is mainly selections from
four earlier books, there are nearly fifty new poems as well. We thus

have, again, the equivalent of something like three collections the size and weight of the earlier collections, and in this case the group begins and ends with a series of poems responding to and accompanied by paintings. Again then it seems reasonable to treat these books as a distinct period.

There is another interesting innovation in this period. The *Later Poems* starts its section of new poems with five pieces considerably longer than anything Thomas published since 'The Airy Tomb' and 'The Minister' thirty years before. None of these is as long as either of those two poems (the five together occupy eighteen pages) but they are markedly different from them. All but one are groups of clearly separated passages; the passages are separated in fact by subtitles or numbers. The effect in each case is of the poem's subject being considered from separate perspectives or angles, rather than the whole poem being a linear progress. Indeed one of the poems, about aspects of Wales through the centuries, makes the point very clearly, for it is called 'Perspectives'. The poem moves through history, but the whole emphasis is on diverse ways of looking at the matter.

I take this new perspectival approach, then, as to both paintings and other topics, as well as its greater diversity, to be characteristic of this whole period. This should not be exaggerated, for Thomas's poems of any period are invariably recognizable as his. Nevertheless there is some extension in the modes of writing and an increased use of line indentation, as in 'Sleight', 'The Tree' and several others. This is most marked in 'The Presence'. More important still would seem to be this perspectival stance along with a certain relaxing of attitude within the poet's cognitive interests. By this I mean the ordinary modes of knowledge; science, music, philosophy and others.

These interests of course had long been present in Thomas's work. Previously, however, there was a certain clenching of grip, or even inhibition, about them; a grip which enabled their rendering in poetry to be the more marked. The symbol – but a very immediate and engulfing one – of Eve as the woman who both tempts to freedom but then entraps, had been inseparable from this. In this later period however a release has been achieved from this long journey and its compulsions. The pressing landscape of the small parish in Wales of the first period has gone. So has the uncertainty and casting about for direction of the second period. So has the facing up to a resolution of this in the search for God in the third period. In this later fourth period R.S. Thomas does not have to cast about for subjects. He finds them readily with an openness and new ease. The old sternness is there too, but it is not everywhere. It is more interested in more things, more resigned, and more philosophical. Thomas's retirement from the living at Aberdaron in 1978 – though he continued to live there – and from full-time service as a priest of the church altogether, seems an obvious occasion for long-latent interests to surface poetically and, in one sense, with easier detachment. In rather different fashion, and mainly through its central concentration on the natural world which was always present, the prose work *A Year in Llyn* also records this general change. Whatever the truth of that, if the journey to this point has been like a strong river, we have now come to its delta.

As has been said, the period begins with a marked change and surprise. This is one of the chief functions of the first set of painting-poems, the 'Impressions'. They deliberately follow hard upon the resolution of *Frequencies*, and tell us to expect an entirely new profile. Thomas's wife Mildred Elsi Eldridge, who died in 1991, was a professional painter and illustrator, and the poet had from time to time used an extended metaphor from painting in earlier poems, for example 'A Priest to His People' in *Song at the Year's Turning* and 'The View from the Window' in *Poetry for Supper*. There have also been a number of occasional poems on individual paintings, for example by Souillac in *The Bread of Truth* and Veneziano in *Laboratories of the Spirit*. All of this emphasizes a theme we have seldom been far from; namely that Thomas is a looking, even a staring poet. To make a concerted response, however, to a large group of paintings as the poet now does with 'Impressions', is to delineate this looking in a new way, establish it as of a different order. In staring at peasant and landscape in the early work, Thomas seemed compelled toward irremovable aspects of the human and natural world. These aspects entailed an inner presence or life of growth, birth and death, and often intolerable drudgery and suffering and endurance. But the poet is now looking at objects deliberately made to be looked at. It is in this light that we can understand, not only why paintings, but why this particular kind of painting, the French Impressionist, was chosen.

French Impressionism made its impact on the art world at a time when old certainties about essential and inner reality were breaking to pieces. In French philosophy Husserl, Merleau-Ponty and

Bergson were among those who wrote of a world in which, it was felt, what the senses apprehend is all that is reliable. Without consciously taking these beliefs on board the French Impressionists, equally, attempted to render snatches or glimpses of the everyday world. This approach exactly matches that of these corresponding philosophers. For, in them, the second half of the nineteenth century saw in France the rise of a phenomenological philosophy; that is to say, a philosophy of appearances. Wallace Stevens, increasingly one of Thomas's mentors in this period, was also influenced by this phenomenology; it clearly marks his poetry of surfaces. In the paintings these glimpses were, precisely, 'impressions', brilliant capturings through a wide range of colours and lights of the surfaces of natural and man-made things. It is not surprising that a reaction soon set in, and that a solid core of inner reality was thought to have been omitted; and it is the more remarkable that R.S. Thomas should have reversed this process. For, having sought the unseekable nature of nothing less than the heart of reality itself (God), or at least an articulation of our approach to that, the poet suddenly turns to the immediate world of surfaces and appearance. And he does this most notably for objects which, as we have said, exist precisely and in one sense only to be looked at. Man-made objects such as fine buildings or good china are also designed, in part, with a view to their appearance; but the painting is that object which isolates its viewing as its inescapable mode of apprehension, its *raison d'etre*. The question is of what Thomas made of this world of appearance.

One cannot answer this question without seeing each painting in full colour next to each poem. One cannot stress this too strongly. (Fortunately the set is easily available in a paperback edition, in print, of the book Thomas himself used, although the latest editions are rather different from the 1958 one. The book is edited by Germain Bazin and is listed in the bibliography at the end of this book.) Because Impressionism captures appearance it is an art not of ideas, or even of harmonious balance, but of colour and light. But it is not merely that one needs the full colour as information. One needs the feeling, the experience of the painting as colour, present at the moment of reading the poem in each case. The paintings energize and fire the poems, and the poems are limp and lifeless without them. This, needless to say, is no criticism of the poems, any more than it would be derogatory of a piece of music to say that one needs instruments to play it. For the poet too is giving 'impressions', entering the painting and its impressionistic spirit, and in many cases taking on the painting's visual image by his own verbal one. The sequence's title, 'Impressions', thus has a double significance.

There are good examples of this in both the portraits and the landscape scenes. In 'Mademoiselle Dihau at the Piano' by Degas, the lady has her back to us but looks at us over her left shoulder. The strong red of the lips at the picture's centre is supported by dots of red in her head dress, and all of this is powerfully contrasted by vast spaces of dark brown and blue of dress, hair and piano itself. Appearing from behind her face is a large expanse of the musical score, propped for playing. The poet's first two impressions come at once: "Asking us what she shall play? But she is her own/music...". His response to the distinctness of the face against the rest is a possible action:

> Almost
> we could reach out a hand
> for the mellow-fleshed,
> sun-polished fruit
> that she is.

He changes his mind, seeing more, but the mode of depiction of this is still the I same:

> But her eyes
> are the seeds of a tart
> apple, and the score a notice
> against trespassing upon
> land so privately owned.

The pun on "tart" is only latent, for the eyes in the picture do indeed push out like apple seeds, and the idea of the music as a warning notice is, again, left as a suggestion or impression, not pushed further. The poem ends there.

In 'The Bridge at Maincy' by Cezanne, the rigidity of a small bridge over a dark river is rendered powerfully horizontal in that nearly all the painting's other main lines are verticals; narrow tall trees close to each other, and the bridge structure's uprights. Thus Thomas's opening question, "Has a bridge to be crossed?", while speculative in one reading, can only get to that via a response to a sensation of an appearance. It is given force by the painting itself at the joint moment of reading and seeing at once. Having then suggested that the bridge is best seen "awaiting/the traveller's return...to his place/at the handrail", the poet adds his own brush-stroke, his own impressionistic surface touch, by seeing that traveller's face as reflected in the murky water as a "water-lily". This image is already in the painting in the form of the moon's reflection ("the waxen/moon from among the clouds"). This continuing of the painting in its own mode is endemic to the nature of these poems, both their dependence and their success.

The impressions the poet adds to and passes on are of different kinds. Sometimes it is a brief list, the painting continued in words. This occurs in the poem on Pissarro's 'Landscape at Chaponval'. In the poem on Van Gogh's famous 'Portrait of Dr Gachet' the poet sees "the eyes like quinine", shimmering and watery as they are; but he also notices how the doctor "listens/to life", an image that picks up the way the figure rests his cheeks on his arms and elbow, as though using the telephone. There is thus both an aural and a visual suggestion, underlying the apprehension of life by the sense first and foremost. In the poem on Toulouse-Lautrec's 'Jane Avril Dancing' the inference is moral; but no judgement is made, it is still impressionistic. The watching middle-aged couple are "all up to the neck/in their conventions" because they are wearing stiff collars to shirt and dress; the girl on the other hand is "showing the knees/by which some would gain entrance to heaven". Occasionally the moral seems drawn out unwarrantedly, as in the poem on Degas's 'Absinthe'. There the poet draws several inferences as to what the woman is thinking and feeling, without attending himself to the painting's very pointed diagonal structure of tables which burst out of the painting's own boundaries. (This is supported by the man's staring out of the painting to its right, he himself already close to that right-hand edge.) The poem feels a little thought-out, and as a result seems to move away from its source.

In other poems Thomas takes the painting's meaning further, but always through its colour and light, through the surface we are given. Strong patches of isolated red are found in many Impressionist paintings, and Thomas senses two as blood. In Cassat's 'Young Woman Sewing' it is menstrual (Thomas puns on "period"), a sensation taken from the large mass of swimming, underwater bluish colour which makes the girl's dress and is two third of the entire painting's area. The blood-red flowers round her are pushed to the edge, yet also contain her, making for an absence of action which Thomas's first stanza seems to follow:

> Sewing. Is she one
> Of the three fates, the first,
> Perhaps, presiding over
> A far birth, her fingers
>
> As though they would join together
> What her brows parted?

The static participle, the "fates" and the birth as distant take on the painting's curious indoor rendering of infertility. In Toulouse-Lautrec's 'Justine Dieuhl', a single blob of bright vermilion for the woman's neckerchief contrasts the soft blue, green and mauve which make up the rest of the picture. For the poet this is "art leading/modesty astray". The point is not there pursued, for we are directed back at once to "the hands,/large enough for encircling/the waist's stem", again with a slight moral and sexual inference, but through the physical, through what is apparent. In two other poems it is the hands that detain the poet's attention; Degas's 'Woman Ironing' (the one painting reproduced in full colour in *Between Here and Now*) and in Manet's 'The Balcony'.

However, most revealing are the several occasions when the poet seems to ask what is beyond the physical, that is to say, what all this physicality itself leads to. This is often very direct, at the start of a poem. The poem on Monet's 'The Bas-Breau Road' begins:

> Who bothers
>   where this road goes?

Confronted with the painting in monochrome, one feels like asking, who indeed? But in face of the full and varied quality of the greens that make them, the question suggests the power of the present trees, leaves and road surface to retain attention on the road itself while still not being able to forget that a road, like anything else, has an inner essence: in the road's case, it goes somewhere. The poem 'The Balcony', already mentioned, makes the contrast more explicitly:

> We watch them. They watch
> What? The world passes,

They remain, looking
As they were meant to do

At a spectacle
Beyond us.

Yet the poem then adds nothing further at all but an 'impression' of each of the three figures:

One stares
as at her fortune
being told. One's hands
are together as if
in applause. The monsieur surmounts
them in sartorial calm.

In the poem on Monet's 'The Gare Saint-Lazare' the poet begins similarly:

The engines
are ready to start,
but why travel
where they are aimed
at?

These questions seem to summarize the large question that impressionism imposes. The physical appearance is mysterious, and not mere stuff or matter, yet it detains us through its palette of colour and light. But these questions also show where the poet is delineating the boundaries of what he is attempting. The poems in each case are adequate to the painting; no more, no less. They are delightful accompaniments to the paintings, so long as the paintings, too, are themselves apprehended at the moment of reading. The poems are thus valuable to anyone looking at the paintings for their own sake. In the context of an appraisal of R.S. Thomas, however, they mark the step taken in the act of looking, after the theologically orientated poetry of the earlier period. They are impressions of impressions, and that mode of apprehension of reality is entered upon by this very visual poet only so far as its own boundaries allow it. It was perhaps a necessity after the earlier period.

The collection *Ingrowing Thoughts* is an epistemological advance on the 'Impressions'. That is to say, it recognizes what happened by

virtue of the delightful but short-lived Impressionist period. In that
period, trust in only physical appearance took the painters not
merely to appearance alone, but in the end, to paint, palette and
brush-stroke alone. It is noteworthy that *Ingrowing Thoughts*,
although about modern painting, includes not one abstract painting.
The way to further human knowledge is not through pure colour,
shape and line. It is still through an apprehension of the physical
world. This time however it is through violently disturbing and dis-
ordering the physical world. There is a strong sexuality in *Ingrowing
Thoughts*, stronger than could be found simply by recording impressions of Parisian women as was done earlier. But this sexuality is still
tied closely to the matter of knowledge, including scientific knowledge, and the appraising, by that, of the universe a corner of which
we inhabit. Horizons and limits, some violent upheaval, the mathematical and the mindless, are captured in the paintings. This time
however the poet does not simply continue them in their own mode.
He combats them and is intrigued by them, and is forced beyond
them because what they show is not literal.

The first poem and the title poem introduce the matter well
enough. The first poem is about Picasso's 'Guernica'. Because
objects in it are arranged quite beyond anything found in the real
world, the poet is constrained to imagine, interpret and project:

> The day before
>   it was calm.
> In the days after
>   a new masterpiece
> was born of the imagination's wandering
>   of the smashed city.
> What but genius can reassemble
>   the bones' jigsaw?

By implication the poet too must use genius to reassemble the
pieces. Thomas's conclusion contains visually apprehended objects,
but sorts them so that the violence that led to their break-up has an
imaginative meaning that makes sense:

> The whole is love
> in reverse. The painter
> has been down at the root
>   of the scream and surfaced

again to prepare the affections
for the atrocity of its flowers.

The final phrase, though neither a literal truth nor an exact physical depiction, is not as such surrealist. Rather, the poet has shown
he will pursue new knowledge in the space left by the violent break-
up (shown in Picasso's painting) of what a traditional world had
agreed it understood. In the painting 'The Red Model' by Magritte,
we see a fence of wooden horizontal planks without gaps between
them. In front of this on the ground is a pair of boots which, disturbingly, merge into human feet and toes. In face of this the poet
is forced to construct the body which the painting's shape and size
suggest should be there, wearing the boots and in some way being
part of them. He cannot do this (except to presume it dead), and is
left therefore with the boots which must have been too small for the
wearer, whose ghost however will

> walk
onward for ever against
an ingrowing thought.

If what we wear – ideas and conventions as well as clothes – is too
small for us, our minds turn inward, like an ingrowing toenail. This
however need not be entirely hopeless, for "ingrowing thoughts" can
also mean thoughts that grow in our minds, that have potential and
life. In the rest of the collection the poet explores and expands the
embryos of thoughts that the images taken from strange paintings
generate in his own thinking, again as a source of new perspectives
on the world.

The poems relating to sex – and there are several – all suggest a
variant on the traditional garden of Eden story, by virtue of which
Eve's sin led to (unlawful) human knowledge. But in these poems
the position is reversed. For the new presence of sex, certainly of
woman, means a distraction from knowledge. In the poem on
Matisse's 'Portrait of a Girl in a Yellow Dress', the woman faces the
"public" and "challenges it to prefer her to the view". In the painting she is central, and largely blocks a big window; and "the
draught/cannot put out/her flame". In the poem on Derain's
'Portrait of Madame Renou' the poet is intrigued, perhaps nearly
captivated, by the woman's smouldering expression, even though
she is thought to spurn not invite. Yet she is 'Madame', married,

and this information battles with the body's urges. The conclusion, if cryptic, takes us beyond the sensual:

> Art like
> this could have left her tagged surname out.

"Could have", not "should have"; the possibilities are left open in art, but not in the conventions of marriage. In the poem on Soutine's 'The Maid of Honour', the ugly woman who is left "intact because no one/challenges it" is powerless to prevent "life's dance" continuing. This wallflower enables a grim extension of meaning on the traditional *virgina intacta* of Christianity.

In three other poems the woman is named as Eve though in none of the paintings is this necessarily implicit. The paintings are those by Bauchant, Chagall and Dali. In Chagall's painting a colossal vase of flowers in which lie two lovers, dwarfs a bridge and river designated by Thomas as "the river of knowledge". In the Dali called 'Drawing' the woman has a chest of drawers instead of breasts. Open, they are seen to be empty, for Thomas "the emptiness/of Eve's ruse". For a feminist era, the implication is decidedly ambivalent.

What then does this leave us in the book's remaining poems. Oversimplifying no doubt, it is a matter of horizons, spaces in which the mind might wander, in danger of a perpetual blankness unless the sense of horizon is itself grasped. The most explicit poem on this theme is on John Selby Bigge's painting 'Composition'. This, though done in a curiously geometric style, is a not far from literal seascape with a schooner entering in the distance from the right-hand margin, and large dangerous crystal-like rock in the foreground. It is important that the rocks themselves look like the sails on a large schooner. The poet writes:

> In the foreground the wreckage
> of the old world, tossed
> spars, agitated waters,
>   reefs, shoals –
>   nobody to blame.
>
> The schooner urges the horizon
> to admit the fallacy
> of its frontiers.

The poem finishes by pointing out directly to the painter that he omitted to put "look-outs" on the schooner in the distance. This is a strange, compelling poem, about the nature of reality and our knowledge of it. Somewhere in the distance a man-made object (the schooner) is seemingly aware of the ambiguous nature of the edges of what we know; yet no humans avail themselves of this knowledge, even though we are not "to blame" for what has happened much nearer to our understanding. Something similar is found in the poem on Paul Nash's 'Encounter in the Afternoon'. This painting is also recognizably a seascape, but with a chessboard pattern across the whole and two objects, perhaps living creatures or perhaps sculptures, in the foreground. Again we are faced with "identity's/absence", a phrase reminiscent of the concerns of Thomas which culminated in *Frequencies*; and again the ominous nature of 'horizons' is explicitly made oppressive.

It is difficult to convey the sense of cognitive interest the collection gives. As said already, R.S. Thomas is in the terrain of knowledge so wide-open, of possibilities so general, once the mess of twentieth century existence has been cleared away, that they can only be groped for tentatively, whether in poetry or in the graphic arts. The collection ends however with a sharp shock, in the shape of a poem about a drawing by Diana Brinton Lee called 'Drawing by a Child'. The drawing imitates the sort of drawing one sees pinned up in primary schools; but the accompanying poem, and its position at the end of the collection, is uncompromising. Thomas begins:

> All of them, Mummy and Daddy
> in their various disguises –
> > it is my revenge on them
> > for bringing me to be.

He ends:

> And horns, horns for everything
> in my nursery, pointing to the
> cuckold I know my father to be.

One is left, after all these poems on paintings, to ask how a poem so unpleasant can be positive, as indeed seems to be the case.

Of what does its positive qualities consist? Why does it conclude this collection, and indeed this whole period? How is it that paintings

have so accommodated a poet – an artist in words – in his search
for and clear openness to new perspectives on the world? How has
it emerged from the now distant hill country of Wales, of poor
Prytherch, the near-sighted muck farmers and those odious English
tourists? Most important, who is the "father"?

This last question can take us back to the first of the five longer
poems with which the *Later Poems* began. It will be remembered that
Later Poems was published between the two books containing the
sequences on paintings, which it has seemed best to discuss
together. The first long poem in the *Later Poems* is called 'Salt', and
it is one of the few poems in the Thomas *oeuvre* before his final
period where, taken at face value, there is any substantial direct
information about someone in the poet's family. Thomas's father,
who was a merchant seaman, is depicted as having conceived a
yearning to travel and sail when young. The poem stands out clearly
in this part of Thomas's later work. The voyages which resulted
from the sailor's ambition are briefly described, along with his return
to marriage to a vicar's daughter and the contrasting confines of a
home in Wales after a life exploring such extensive horizons.

From then on the poem describes the sailor's attitudes; discon-
tent, yearning for the past, and a curious puzzlement; a failure to
take command in his post-nautical life:

> The voice of my father
> in the night with the hunger
> of the sea in it and the emptiness
> of the sea. While the house founders
> in time, I must listen to him
> complaining, a ship's captain
> with no crew, a navigator
> without a port; rejected
> by the barrenness of his wife's
> coasts...

The poet goes on to refer to his father's "weak smile...the lack of
understanding of life...out of touch with the times", The whole is
permeated with the skilful proliferation of metaphor which, by now,
we take to be the organic heart of this poet's mode of expression,
and of his poetic imagination. This time life at sea itself makes the
metaphor continuous. But the end is a surprise:

> And I,
> can I accept your voyages
> are done; that there is no tide
> high enough to float you off
> this mean shoal of plastic
> and trash? Six feet down,
> and the bone's anchor too
> heavy for your child spirit
> to haul on and be up and away?

Rhetorical question is common in Thomas's poetry; yet there are far fewer such questions in these later poems. All the more remarkable, then, is this spate of questions at the end of this clearly biographical poem, and one speculates on what is meant by them. One senses the poet missing a father's love, a phrase still ambiguous; there is a wistfulness in the poem's ending, as though only now late in his own life can the poet lay a ghost, express what was previously inexpressible. But the same phrase ("can I accept your voyages are done...?") suggests that the haunting presence of the father, here touched on in so many ways, has accompanied the poet through his own work. To put it another way, here at last, unlike Milton's Satan, Thomas acknowledges origins; and by that means he attains both a resignation and an easement of burden which is characteristic of several poems in this latest period. It is an important moment when a creative artist makes such a step explicit.

It is achieved furthermore only in a long poem, by repeatedly rubbing it in (the title, characteristically, has a double meaning), and the way is open for further expansiveness. The second longer poem, 'Plas Difancoll', though interesting enough, is not so exceptional; but the third is called 'Perspectives'. The title itself summarizes the new approach. The poem is in five sections, each about a period in the history of Wales. Each section is sub-titled: 'Primeval', 'Neolithic', 'Christian', 'Mediaeval' and 'Modern'. 'Mediaeval' beautifully captures a feeling of the Wales of the bards:

> Sing me, my lord said,
> the things nearer home:
> my falcons, my horse.

Yet the section 'Neolithic' is perhaps the most distinctive, and most shows what this different approach is achieving. It is voiced as

though by a disgruntled neolithic reactionary who finds no pleasure
in the new technology round him ("Wheels go no faster than what
pulls them"), and doubts if a hoped-for return to the past will
happen:

> This
> plucked music has come
> to stay. The natural breathing
> of the pipes was to
> a different god. Imagine
> depending on the intestines
> of a polecat for accompaniment
> to one's worship!

The satire is easily applied to our own time. But, appearing as it
does in a much longer poem than usual, it is far less terse than
Thomas is usually. The poem does not combine political stance and
national symbol with an impact essentially brief. Rather, it takes a
wider view as from a distance, and from different angles; in short,
different perspectives. Here we realize that each of these sections
could have stood as poems alone, like the short poems in all
Thomas's previous books. And in hindsight, we see that the same
was true of 'Salt', even though there the sections were not formally
marked off at all. For example, the passage from "Later/the letters
began:..." down to "...the soft fire/that would destroy him" could be
read as a separate poem not unlike 'The Letter' in *Poetry for Supper*,
and the passage "Suddenly he was old..." down to "...the anachronism of his view", published under a title such as 'Sailor', might well
have been equally indistinguishable from other short poems as to its
source. This again is a marked change. What Thomas is doing here
is mitigating the sting of his earlier impact without, however, writing in the extended mode derived by most modern poets from the
ordinary tradition of the hexameter. It is as though there is a willingness to allow that thoughts about great and weighty things (here,
Wales) are not to be expressed only as from intense pressure. They
are, or feel, both quieter and more distended. The new mode of
longer sequences will re-appear more than once in Thomas's final
period, considered later in chapter 5.

In 'Covenanters', there are six sections respectively called 'Jesus',
'Mary', 'Joseph', 'Lazarus', 'Judas Iscariot' and 'Paul'. Again, by
deliberately placing the presumptive main character first, the order

takes away any sense of approach to climax or resolution. All six sections furthermore are distinct in poetic form. The first is one of the poet's many short pieces of irregular line length, with no rhyme or endstop, and a quasi-stanza division in the middle. The second has seven three-line stanzas of very short lines. The third is like the first, but with very short lines and spoken as though by Joseph himself. The fourth has two stanzas, each with four longer lines. The fifth is like the first but, disturbingly, devoid of any punctuation until the final full-stop, as though to deprive Judas of the give and take of ordinary human communication. The sixth poem is the longest and addresses Paul in the voice of the poet himself.

Since the writing is not so much new as newly arranged, it feels as if we are being invited to look again at the nature of Thomas's writing itself. The poems – or sections – are no less compelling than in earlier books. To the crowd's question about a future life Jesus answers in this fashion:

> It is here,
> he said, tapping his forehead
> as one would to indicate
> an idiot.

The combination of 'the kingdom of God is within you" (*Luke* xvii 21) with the Pauline view of Christianity as "unto the Greeks, foolishness" (I *Corinthians* i 23) could hardly be more economically, vividly or naturally expressed. In an intriguing insight Judas is seen as "genuinely/hurt by a certain extravagance/in the Master", while to Paul the poet's play with two words is as dry as ever: "For instance, I like you/on love". Yet scarcely any link between the characters as part of a single gospel narrative is offered. Not that it is denied either; but the reader is left to provide such links and to make any required inferences.

The fifth poem of this group of longer poems has the most explicit use of this method. It is called 'Thirteen Blackbirds Look At A Man', and this echoes Wallace Stevens's poem 'Thirteen Ways of Looking At A Blackbird'. This echo is matched by a parallel form, there being thirteen short numbered sections in Thomas's poem, none longer than seven lines. Broadly we are in a garden, looked at from the blackbirds' point of view, and the word 'man' appears once and no more in each section. Here are three sections:

4

We have eaten
the blackberries and spat out
the seeds, but they lie
glittering like the eyes of a man.

5

After we have stopped
singing, the garden is disturbed
by echoes; it is
the man whistling, expecting
everything to come to him.

6

We wipe our beaks
on the branches
wasting the dawn's
jewellery to get rid
of the taste of a man.

On one possible reading of the poem, there is an underlying mythical or historical movement. This would go from an opening section
in, again, the garden of Eden, to the final section questioning
whether 'man' will be present when the birds return, 'man' having,
perhaps, destroyed himself by nuclear war or some other holocaust.
But this is only one possible reading, among others. Eden is hinted
at again as late as section nine ("In the cool/of the day...", echoing
Genesis iii 8), but by then "man" has already "had his licence
endorsed/thirteen times", presumably in trying to overtake the birds
in flight. But Genesis isn't the only non-Stevens echo, with "the
garden is disturbed by echoes" itself echoing both T.S. Eliot's
'Burnt Norton' and Shakespeare's *The Tempest*. The poem is whim-
sical in something like the Stevens manner, yet chilling too in its
impact; and we see the eerily, monosyllabically evoked "man" from
the viewpoint of creatures to whom, as we know, this poet has
devoted attention and interest for a lifetime. There is a strange
silence and absence across the poem's garden; but this is not the
absence of God found in the earlier period of Thomas's writing. An
old myth is being reworked and inverted, but also looked at again,

and the blackbirds' perceptions are ways of seeing within a cosmos strangely unchanging in its ultimate, unknown nature.

These five longer poems are arranged in an order of decreasing pressure. They touch on topics which have long mattered to Thomas perhaps more than any, yet the pressure is gradually allayed. This again is a notable new tone in Thomas's writing as he grows older, and he is doing something new, or at least differently. Now that the religious consummation has been tentatively reached, or certainly its poetic expression, a philosophical filling-out is possible. The arrangement of cognate poems as sections in a tentative larger whole – both these five longer poems and the two groups of poems about paintings – takes both poet and reader back a step, and we can recognize this larger process at work. But even more, this may be the lightening, perhaps the healing, of what many have long sensed to be a profound hurt in Thomas.

We have referred to this already in passing. It appears that this hurt surfaced in the poet at a very early point in his career. Some of the earliest uncollected poems in the Anglo-Welsh magazines lack the incisive and tight-lipped economy which soon became the R.S. Thomas hallmark along with his metaphoric power. Whether it was the condition of Wales, the brutalizing of the language he was forced to use through chance of birth, the final post-war decline in the influence of the priesthood, the recognition of the import of a family relationship, or some more personally inward inhibition, is best considered by reference to his autobiographical prose writing which was first published in 1997 (see bibliography). But the remaining shorter poems in *Between Here and Now* and the *Later Poems* continue many of Thomas's usual themes and emphases but at times with, I feel, a slightly altered tone. It is as if he need no longer feel this pain, whether its deepest origin was outward or inward. As a result, in 'Gradual', which appears almost at once after the five longer poems just discussed, Thomas can say:

> I have come to the borders
> of the understanding. Instruct
> me, God, whether to press
> onward or draw back.

The poet does not press on or draw back. This is not to say that he sticks, though as before he sometimes draws aside. Rather, increasingly withdrawing as life goes on, he now repeats and replays and recycles his characteristic themes, symbols and tropes in constantly renewed and surprising combinations.

In *Between Here and Now* and the new poems in *Later Poems*, the now expected tropes of self, bone, glittering glass, music, the "mortgaged" self or principle, the tree, flower, nails into flesh, electricity, and inter-galactic signal, proliferate. Again the feeling of a delta, a spreading out wide, is present. This elaboration of earlier themes is now accompanied by a new explicitness about repetition itself. In the poem 'Flowers', toward the end of *Between Here and Now*, Thomas refers to "that other flower/which is ageless", and writes of it

> that as often
> as it is picked blossoms
> again, that has the perfection
> of all flowers, the purity
> without the fragility.

Although symbols and themes are repeated, they are never dead, never sterile. In this period of Thomas's poetry, one feels often, that as often as it is picked it blossoms again. One could hardly wish to put it better. It feels like an image of poetry, and in this context of Thomas's own. Furthermore the theme of repetition itself seems to insinuate in a number of images. There is for example "the distance/within that the tireless signals/come from" ('The New Mariner"); man's wider contemporary life "recuperating endlessly/in intermissions of the machine" ('Aleph'); and autumn leaves on the ground like glass, "broken repeatedly and/as repeatedly replaced" ('Plas Difancoll").

Yet there are new topics too. As well as the poems on paintings, there are in *Between Here and Now* a skeleton, primitive people, Greece and the Mediterranean, jewellery, more and more aspects of radio communication and sub-atomic physics, letter-writing while on holiday, the concentration camps, and apartment life. One of the most compelling examples, to the present writer at least, is 'Correspondence':

> You ask why I don't write.
> But what is there to say?
> The salt current swings in and out
> of the bay, as it has done
> time out of mind. How does that help?

It leaves illegible writing
on the shore. If you were here,
we would quarrel about it.
People file past this seascape
as ignorantly as through a gallery
of great art. I keep searching for meaning.
The waves are a moving staircase
to climb, but in thought only.
The fall from the top is as sheer
as ever. Younger I deemed truth
was to come at beyond the horizon.
Older I stay still and am
as far off as before. These nail-parings
bore you? They explain my silence.
I wish there were as simple
an explanation for the silence of God.

The figures are renewed as the waves are; always the same, yet
each yielding its fresh new glint and flash of "meaning", "truth"
and "silence" so long as the poet searches for it. By a single word
in each case "swings" and "file" bring a multitude of details before
the eye more surely than would a paragraph of prose. The fall from
the top is as sheer as ever, into a Wordsworthian abyss of secreted
meditation.

A sense of widening perspective, yet the same motifs rewritten;
these are characteristic of these later short poems. One reason why
the poet may be doing this, is that his poetic articulation of God,
reached in *Frequencies*, temporarily at least, has gone as far as it
could upward, and has reached a plateau. A number of poems articulate this, among them 'Covenant', 'One Way', 'Senior', 'The New
Mariner', 'Observation' and 'The Presence' from *Between Here and
Now*, and 'Cadenza' and 'The Tree' from *Later Poems*. In 'One
Way' the poet designates his futuristic mode of prayer:

> God,
> I whispered, refining
> my technique, signalling
> to him on the frequencies
> I commanded,

The frequencies are now "commanded", and the signals go out with
a constancy, even if to "the one station that remained closed". A

metaphysic of probing as now not travel onward but remaining in a
differently conceived space-time is present:

> Where
> to go, when the arrival
> is as the departure? Circularity
> is a mental condition, the
> animals know nothing of it.
>
> ('Covenant')

As a result, although God remains elusive, the reasons for and
nature of his existence, and ours, can be suggested by figures which
do not strain forward but invite contemplation. God was perhaps
"born from our loss of nerve"; he "needs us/as a conductor his
choir"; and we ourselves are perhaps "his penance/for having made
us". More newly, the obscenities of the concentration camps can give
rise to a conceit as remarkable as it seems metaphysically accurate:

> Their wrong is an echo defying
> acoustical law, increasing not fading.
>
> ('Beacons')

Since God can now be characterized again and again from, as it
were, a now still point, it is theologically apt that Christ can begin
to come into focus as the body on the tree. This is touched upon in
'Fair Day', 'Code', 'Forest Dweller', 'Covenanters', 'Carol' and elsewhere. But this is not elaborated. Instead, there comes the different
theme of old age. R.S. Thomas was already nearly seventy when the
first book of this period was published, and a number of poems
make some reference to the passing of the years, although never with
self-pity and seldom as something to dwell on. More often there is
the detachment to which we have already referred, as though the
pursuit is over and "the way on/is over your shoulder". Yeats is an
increasing source of allusion again in this period, and as with Yeats
the ageing poet makes artefacts against time, although with Thomas
a comparison between present and past is the poem's usual source
of attention. The aptly named 'Pluperfect' more than usually renders the past irretrievable, using the book's title rather to relate
present time to present place:

> Where are you? I

shouted, growing old in
the interval between here and now.

It is one of many passages where we hear the echo of an earlier
poem, in this instance the end of 'God's Story' in *Laboratories of the
Spirit*. Yeats's gently singing voice is seldom present; it is Thomas's
own characteristic voice, and often the note of reminiscence seems
sad. Yet it is universal in import too, and the perspective of age
brings purchase on vast sweeps of time. In 'Covenant' the poet
writes, "Seven times have passed over him, and he is still here". The
context makes clear that the reference is to God, yet Thomas's own
threescore and ten seems to hover here. In 'Bent', the profound
sense of centuries of human evolution still leaving no essential
change, is equally impregnated with the poet's own long-cultivated
stoicism:

> Two million years
> in straightening them
>   out, and they are still bent
> over the charts, the instruments,
>   the drawing-board...

Several poems refer to this perspective of age only in passing, a
dry acknowledgement of the inevitable. "The old men ask/for more
time, while the young/waste it" ('Patterns'). " At sixty there are still
fables/to outgrow, the possessiveness/of language" ('Senior'). "It is
so long/since I cooled" ('Inside'). "Forgetting yesterday,/ignorant of
the future,/I take up apartments/in the here and now..." ('Flat').
Rarely, as in 'The New Mariner', is it expanded. Old age is itself a
perspective, a way of reckoning up what has been achieved, or
changed, or disappointed. The fullest poem on this topic is
'Evening', while equally moving is 'Seventieth Birthday', addressed
to the poet's now ailing wife. From the knowingly inadequate bio-
chemist's analysis of her body through an allusion to Yeats on time
passing the conclusion is deeply personal:

> You are drifting away from
> me on the whitening current of your hair.
> I lean far out from the bone's bough,
> knowing the hand I extend
> can save nothing of you but your love.

Perhaps most surprising, so different is the context, are the echoes in this poem of Gerard Manley Hopkins in stanza 18 of 'The Wreck of the Deutschland'. It is nearly Thomas's last poem of this period on the matters of sex, woman and love.

In the poem 'Passage' this theme of old age and the wider passing of historical time are linked. There are five stanzas, each in the first person pronoun, and with the first four identifying with Shakespeare, Donne, Shelley and Yeats respectively. As so often in the later Thomas, a juxtaposition of the life of dead religion with the death of living science occurs, this time in the last stanza; and this time too reaching a historical conclusion the poet can feel is his own:

> I stand now, tolling my name
> in the poem's empty church,
>   summoning to the celebration
>   at which the transplanted
> organs are loth to arrive.

It is a comment on Thomas's poetic stature that he can link his "name" not absurdly with the previous four, and that the 'I' of the poem may be read as either poetry personified or as R.S. Thomas himself. More generally, the theme of history has emerged too as a strong preoccupation in these later poems. This too is enabled by the perspective of old age, as though civilization's past and one's own have become part of the same view of things. They are now perennial from a still point in time the poet has reached.

Several poems survey history, whether as a principle of movement or as time itself embodied, and they use historical events or imagery. In 'Centuries', there are six two-line stanzas, each referring to a century from the fifteenth to the twentieth, and we see the same perspectival approach noted already as a later characteristic, captured here in miniature. 'Aleph' 'Beacons', 'Bent', 'Minor', 'Forest Dwellers', 'Gospel' and 'Requiem' all have this dimension, while 'Contacts' has a comparable division into roles, in this case the Oedipus-figure, the warmonger, the scholar, the sage and the destitute. In the poem itself named 'History' the poet combines a dark image of history's unknown origins with a sense, both positive and pessimistic at once, that its relentlessness is here always:

> It remains unconsoled
> in its dust-storm of tears,

remembering the Crusades,
the tortures, the purges

But time passes by;
it commits adultery
with it to father the cause
of its continued weeping.

So history too is a preoccupation in this period. Yet, because a
certain stillness has been attained, by the consummation of the
probe for God and by the onset of old age itself, this pessimism does
not prevent a more general cognitive attitude from manifesting itself,
a quieter sense of understanding and of knowledge. The staring is
less intense, while the power of perception is undiminished. In this
later period this matter of knowledge is more and more associated
with the symbol of the tree, its uprightness and its greenness. The
symbol is diffuse and its intensity as the place of human blood sacrifice, found toward the end of *Pietà*, is much more muted. The tree
is a focus for the idea of knowledge because it is upright against the
otherwise empty horizon; it has branches, diversity (like a delta too),
and it is green and growing. It is tied still to the tree in the garden
of Eden, and one may note how many of Thomas's poems now, historical in movement, start with Eden and end with galactic space;
but the Eden tree is not the main emphasis. In the poem 'Adagio'

           the poet stands
     beneath leafless trees
           listening to the wind
     bowing on their wires. What
     it affirms is: The way on
           is over your shoulder...

That this leafless tree conversely implies self-imposed human ignorance is underlined by an outstanding later poem, 'The Tree', where
the whole matter is unravelled:

     What we may not
do is to have our horizon bare,
     is to make our way
on through a desert white with the bones
of our dead faiths. It is why,
some say, if there were no tree,

> we would have to set one up
>   for us to linger under,
> its drops falling on us as though to confirm
> he has blood like ourselves.

But, although humans may have learnt this, their modern attempt to
act on it has taken away its maker:

> We have set one up, but
> of steel and so leafless that
>   he has taken himself
> off out of the reach
> of our transmitted prayers.

The poem ends with our equally abortive efforts to re-establish
contact.

It might seem from this that in the applications of science R.S.
Thomas sees a greed for materially useful knowledge taken too far.
However, perhaps that suggestion also goes too far, and it is more
likely that the tree suggests knowledge to any particular extent we
truly need it. This may be misdirected, and indeed dangerous:

> What shall we do
> with the knowledge growing
> into a tree that to shelter
> under is to be lightning struck?
>   ('It')

But the tree grows nonetheless, and that is its nature. Knowledge is
not to be appropriated and greedily exploited, but must not remain
stunted and withered either. Indeed it can generate a surprisingly
libidinous image:

> I have thought often
> of the fountain of my people
> that played beautifully here
> once in the sun's light
> like a tree undressing.
>   ('The Bush')

It is as closely bound to the body, in another religion:

the Buddha
seated cross-legged...

From his navel
the tree grows whose canopy
is knowledge. He counts the leaves

as they fall, that are words
out of the mouth of the unseen
God, washing his thoughts clean
in them.

('Island')

In this later period, then, the tree as both the place of crucifixion
and as source of knowledge both old and modern seem to meet.
Later Poems ends with the short poem 'Prayer', where the connections of poetry, religion and science are made economically explicit:

Baudelaire's grave
not too far
from the tree of science.
Mine, too,
since I sought and failed
to steal from it,
somewhere within sight
of the tree of poetry
that is eternity wearing
the green leaves of time.

This is the image we are left with from this period; the tree,
standing in the bare spaces of the deserted centuries. But this attrac-
tion of Thomas toward the natural and the historical finally raises a
traditional distinction, that between history and philosophy.
Although Thomas clearly has philosophical interests, one would not
say he is primarily a philosophical poet, in the sense that
Wordsworth is, or even T.S. Eliot. Thomas seldom if ever expands
into broad philosophical reflection. He always practised the cut-off
phrase, the terse observations successively listed. He meets the
demands of human, religious or natural event by recording a series
of poetic impulses, each fully charged at the moment of writing, and
vividly and precisely registered. If the matter in hand should be
more abstract in its nature, then it is turned in an elliptical, reserved

phrase of considerable economic force. These features predominate
in R.S. Thomas's later but not final writing, the writing this chapter
has considered. Again and again in this period one notes the characteristic Thomas poem, the kind toward which he had been
working in the previous years of intense theological quest, ending in
Frequencies. There is the brief opening statement or searching
rhetorical question on some passing event or an absorbing spiritual
matter. Then follow the abrupt phrases, further rhetorical questions,
the two or three (usually three) brilliant metaphors, seemingly
achieved with both casualness and penetration at once, and further
short, stabbing reflections. Then comes that long last sentence, often
seven or eight lines in a poem seldom more than three times that
length. In this long sentence the poet seems to wind through and use
up the remainder of his poetic thrust as far as the subject-matter on
each occasion will allow. There are, of course, other forms too,
notably the more regularly-spaced stanza, resulting in a shorter
poem in the nature of an 'aside' again from the main quest. But the
characteristic poem has these features and this long last sentence. As
a result, one does not need a philosophical expansion; or, perhaps,
the rich throbbing of the end draws us into making our own:

> Realising the sound
> returned to us from a flower's
> speaking-trumpet was an echo
> of our own voices, we have switched
> our praise, directing it rather
> at those mysterious sources
> of the imagination you yourself
> drink from, metabolising
> them instantly in space-time
> to become the ichor of your radiation.
>   ('Publicity Inc.')

The absorbed and spaced out final sentence, with its phrases and
images carefully interweaving with each other, stands to the poem
as a whole as this period of writing stands to Thomas's work as a
whole. There is a degree of widening out, just enough to move freely
in, and the poet will not be committed further. After the early periods in which the peasant, village, church and landscape gave the
poet a clear subject, a period of indecision seemed to follow. The
result was the modernist probe into the traces and remains, or the

absence, of God. Through this long process Thomas perfected his poetry as a diversified instrument of communication by which to explore the natural, technological and spiritual worlds he confronted. In this latest period so far Thomas produced poems as strong as any in the earlier periods. 'Correspondence', 'Evening', 'Return', 'Flowers', 'Threshold' and 'The Presence' seem the most newly distinctive in *Between Here and Now*; and in *Later Poems*, apart from the five longer ones already discussed, there are 'The Tree', 'Passage', 'Arrival' and 'Minuet'. Yet it is the qualities right across all the writing that seem most likely to survive, born of the meeting of an intense physical apprehension with an equally intense spiritual struggle. Two or three of the later poems touch on a sense of arrival. 'Arriving' is one, but these and some others name the place of arrival as well; the small country, Wales. This is explicit in 'Minor' and 'The Bush'. In 'Arrival' itself, the event of coming across what you were not seeking is the poem's occasion. This is "the village in the Welsh hills...with no road out/but the one you came in by". The poet

> has arrived
> after long journeying where he
> began, catching this
> one truth by surprise
> that there is everything to look forward to.

This period is equally, if by its nature less frequently, rich in highly charged and original metaphoric power. In this same poem 'Arrival'

> A bird chimes
> from a green tree
> the hour that is no hour
> you know.

One can only admire, and wonder whether "chimes" came from long observation or instant recognition. In other poems, the adder is "a toy necklace/among the weeds and flowers", God has a "cogged smile", and "the lights' jewellery sticks in the throat/of the fish". The lightning goes "scissoring/between clouds", and the poet's buried father lies in the graveyard under a "becalmed/fleet" with its "stone sails". Along with this metaphor in the poetry is the equally frequent

double-entendre; the scarecrow's "loss of face"; the way the poet
has "put/off pride"; and the "divine/cut-out". Many of the poems'
titles are rich with impacted meaning; 'Evening', 'Salt', 'Flat', 'Bent',
'Correspondence'. This power of words in Thomas leads one, again,
to feel the need to characterize poetry's power more generally. How
can mere agility with words give a poem permanent survival-value,
no matter how appalling or desperate the things with which it deals?
It may be that it refreshes one's deepest sense that human communication is in some way worthwhile; that, because such writing and
saying themselves seem to hold a constantly renewed power, then it
must be that existence and its parts, too, have some ultimate value
or significance.

Here is the poem 'Evening', in which the metaphor in the second
stanza and the packed double-meanings of the words in the fourth,
seem to survive the poet's own despondency at his failure in his task:

> From his window he looked out
> on a wood from which
> flocks of birds, many
> as his thoughts, periodically
>
> would erupt. Below him
> the wild swans of the sea
> came drifting in to die
> on the shore. There was no question
>
> of why he was there; he
> was there with the fire
> of sticks and the words that
> over a long life
>
> should have appreciated
> adequately to the purchase
> of the things grown dearer
> in the slow setting of his sun.

V. Final Years

(Experimenting with an Amen 1986, *The Echoes Return Slow* 1988,
Counterpoint 1990, *Mass for Hard Times* 1992,
No Truce with the Furies 1995)

In 1983 R.S. Thomas was seventy. Major poets have sometimes written some of their greatest work after that age, most obviously Sophocles, Hardy and Yeats himself, one of Thomas's major influences on his own testimony. That Thomas would produce at least another five collections in his final years, is something he presumably didn't count on, and if there is a unity in this final group of five collections, it may lie in the sense that pervades them, that any one might have been the last. Of course, poets do not necessarily write poems in the order in which they appear, nor in the groupings that collections place over them. The next book may be nearly complete before the previous one is published. Nor is death the only obstacle. Illness, disinclination or fading powers may all loom ahead. Yet Thomas's cosmic and eschatological concerns might seem to have made him especially aware of all this, while ensuring that the theme was guaranteed just as the life was not. This paradox of material is itself a deep-layer tension behind the unfolding of these final, very important works.

Experimenting with an Amen is already marked with finitude, and not only in its title. It contains nearly seventy poems, more than any book since *Song at the Year's Turning* thirty years earlier. It also at least envisages the journey's end, partly by looking back, but mainly by entering on a territory in which to some extent things of this world are put aside, or are seen from a different perspective, outside of time. The book is remarkable for its removal of a great deal of what previously concerned the poet for so long; more so, in hindsight, in that the next collection *The Echoes Return Slow* would return to those concerns rather explicitly. The title 'Emerging' was used twice, we recall, for poems in Thomas's third, devotional period. Now he had emerged. He inhabits a human body, but it is as though that is now incidental, and a timeless and spiritual realm is now quietly occupied. It is not that any overt suppression of the flesh is now occurring. Rather, the need for any such thing seems over. There is now a certain timelessness and spacelessness, within which mortal vacuum the poet now has an area in which to move without the agitations and relentless inner pressures of earlier periods, even recent periods as in the new poems in *Later Poems*. "I will not/be here long" the poet says, in a curious poem called "The Fly", and the familiar diversity of meanings in the one phrase is significant. The poet may be saying that he was soon to die; or that against the average human span he was necessarily near to that; or equally that any human life, of whatever length, by its nature does not detain us here long and that the perspective of age makes earthly concerns fade away as a matter of course.

In this collection, *Experimenting with an Amen*, sex, money, Wales, tourism, politics and even the galaxy itself are almost entirely absent. Occasionally a Welsh person or scene, a remembered woman or a financial metaphor appear, but as though at a distance, and with less palpable embodiment. Even God himself, trying adversary and elusive stranger, is not present in the same way, although in other ways this collection is a touch more orthodox in Christian terms. These things are not gone for ever and will return in even later books. As the title says, the poet is experimenting, paradoxically taking temporary lodgings in a timeless mode of existence. This relation between time and out-of-time is itself a major strand of the collection. The characteristically vigorous and tangible imagery of former years, including the most recent, gives way to a blurred atmosphere of shadow and light. In 'A Country', the landscape of Wales yields to a placeless place not bound by the earth's spectrum:

> It is nowhere
>   and I am familiar
> with it as one is
> with a song...
> No sun
> rises there, so there is no sun
> to set. It is the mind
> suffuses it with a light
>   that is without
>   shadows.

In 'Destinations', 'The Bank', 'This One' and 'Where?' the same light is evinced. In this light and its puzzlement the late R.S. Thomas asked his late questions.

These questions proliferate, just as they did at the start of the poet's career. Now however they are no longer the strenuous, angry challenging questions of that time. But they are not the deliberately gauged questions of *Frequencies* either. This does not mean they are world-weary, and they are only regretful in a wide and philosophical context. They are sometimes a touch wistful. The preponderance of this later formulating of questioning is often made clear by the titles: 'Questions', 'Asking', 'Reply'; and in 'The Wood', a mass of questions in which a man, in a wood, clearly cannot see it for the trees:

A wood.
A man entered;
thought he knew the way
through. The old furies
attended. Did he emerge
in his right mind? The same
man? How many years
passed? Aeons? What is
the right mind? What does
"same" mean? No change of clothes
for the furies? Fast
as they are cut down
the trees grow, new
handles for axes.

Dante's mid-life crisis, famously expressed as his losing of his way and entering a dark forest, here becomes the late-civilization analytical worrying of a Wittgenstein. Yet "no change of clothes for the furies?" anticipates the title of an even later collection. The poem ends on the same questioning note. One gets no impression that R.S. Thomas expects answers, or even that he now regrets the fact. Rather he is recapitulating the mode of his poetic work. Every moment of life is a pressure, a perception, a question, and in such a way that a further extension can always be found, a further image or phrase, or yet another poem, another turning of that idea to a new facet. "How many times/over must he begin again?" the poem ends, and we recall that mode of renewal toward the end of *Later Poems*. It is as though the approach has itself now been raised to a level outside of its employment in ordinary life.

A few poems are explicitly retrospective. 'A Poet', 'Biography', 'Sarn Rhiw', 'Strands', 'Retirement' and 'A Life' are on this theme. Paradoxically, they function to retain our sense of the poet's hold on this life rather than his removal toward something other. Yet even these have a generality of reference that survives even the cases where physical embodiments of this world are alluded to. 'A Poet' ends thus:

> Patron without condescension
> of the art, he teaches flight's
> true purpose, which is,
> sensitive but not too blinded
> by some inner radiance, to be
> in delicatest orbit about it.

The poet has not lost the power of the striking image. Prayers are "like gravel/flung at the sky's/window", and, in returning the unsolicited bad poems of a stranger:

>   "These are great
> poems", I write, and see heaven's
> slums with their rags flying,
> cripples brandishing their crutches,
> and the one, innocent of scansion,
> who knows charity is short
> and the poem for ever, suffering
> my dark lie with all the blandness
> with which the round moon suffers an eclipse.
>   ('Unposted')

But these occasions are rare. It is not that Thomas was no longer in touch with the physical or natural world. Rather, it seems he has absorbed its manifestations for so long, that they are now suffused across his writing as general reference, even environment; and he chooses not to multiply them metaphorically further. Painting is a continuing subject, as in 'Gallery'; but only generally, and no one painting is encountered. Only the bone, mirror and embodiments of modern science remain, as well as the Welsh landscape where the poet lived, in the Lleyn peninsula. It becomes harder to group poems according to topic or type. The long last sentence, as in 'Andante' and 'Cones', is strongly in evidence. Sometimes a poem feels like the rewriting of an earlier one, as here with 'Aubade' and

'Moorland', the latter evidently a remembering of the famous poem
'The Moor' in *Pietà*, but here with its surprising end.

Finally then, this collection is suffused with a new sense of the
timeless. Poem after poem seems to escape any sense of the present
moment, of the pressure of incident, scene or person. 'Roles', 'Gift',
'A Country', 'Andante', 'West Coast', 'Zero', 'Song', 'Similarities',
'Destinations', 'Ritual', 'Countering', 'The Fly', 'Gallery' and even
'April Song' are among those which seem immersed in this preoccupation and to emerge from it and in it. Time is not always alluded
to specifically in each of these, and it is the removal of what is
referred to from time's process that is often so evident. However, in
'Zero' the subject is explicit:

> What time is it?
>   Is it the hour when the servant
> of Pharaoh's daughter went down
>   and found the abandoned baby
> in the bulrushes? The hour
>   when Dido woke and knew Aeneas
> gone from her? When Caesar
>   looked at the entrails and took
> their signal for the crossing
>   of the dividing river?
>   Is it
> that time when Aneirin
>   fetched the poem out of his side
> and laid it upon the year's altar
>   for the appeasement of envious
> gods?
>   It is no time
> at all. The shadow falls
>   on the bright land and men
> launder their minds in it, as
>   they have done century by
> century to prepare themselves for the crass deed.

No doubt the poet was feeling his age too; but the deceptively
simple request in the first line, apparently for the time of day on the
clock, leads to a cumulating sense of how even major mythical and
historical events do no more than show that time itself always lasts
far longer still, to the point where it cannot be measured.

Within this late timelessness there is a feeling, a touch, of something nearer the orthodox doctrinally, here and there in this book. But it isn't just positive or optimistic. In context those terms would sound shallow. Rather the poet seems to immerse himself into those modes of discourse unencumbered by alternative temptations, or necessary knowledge of human daily existence. 'Testimonies' is a perspectival poem of warped or failed responses to Christ's presence in human affairs. The most direct poem of this kind however, and I feel one of the book's central statements, is 'Hebrews 12.29'. The biblical verse named is the last in its chapter and something of a surprise when you consult it. The poet teases out the implications, facing that the perceptive seeing with which he began his poetic career has switched from peasants and landscape through science and art to God himself, still finding no ultimate correlative, in reality, for language. He faces with resignation that endlessly producing poem after poem can articulate only our time-bound position. "We have stared, and stared, and not stared/truth out", and the name of God appears and disappears.

Yet this, too, is not the last impression the book leaves with us. From a poet so often called terse, harsh, and pessimistic, we have in the poem 'Countering' a verse which suggests that all along there has been a hope hovering, even if its articulation can hardly go further than gentle, formal request. If indeed R.S. Thomas was to "not be here long" then the final two-and-a-half lines could one day stand as an epigraph for his life, work and influence:

> Then take my hand that is
> of the bone the island
> is made of, and looking at
> me say what time it is
> on love's face, for we have
> no business here other than
> to disprove certainties the clock knows.

From such finalities the poet, surviving after all, might well have found himself in open spaces as to what was to be said next. All the more contrasting then was the outcome, *The Echoes Return Slow*, three years later in 1988. For on the face of it – whatever more than that remains to consider – the new collection is strikingly autobiographical. This is in tune with the wider willingness to declare himself in this period, outside of his poetry, we have already noted. The collection's reaction to the timeless is itself part of the cyclical rhythm which the poet couldn't avoid if the endless production of poem after poem was to be given life. The collection takes the reader through the stages of the poet's life, real, imagined, fleetingly recalled, or constructed. It consists of pairs of alternating prose pieces and poems, to left and right, respectively on each open double page. There are sixty-three pairs. The first five pairs derive from the poet's birth and childhood in Cardiff and Anglesey and the next five from youth and student years in Bangor. After a flower-poem interlude (page 23) he is in his first parish of Manafon for five more, and in the seventeenth poem (page 35) his first and only child is conceived.

Aspects of family, parish and Welsh rural life then interweave with a deepening awareness of the numinous absence of what his vocation has led him to propagate to his congregations. Briefly the early shepherds of the Prytherch years reappear, but the previous book's barrier of timelessness intervenes and the new self-examination leads to a more general metaphor. This is the sea. The sea has appeared sporadically throughout, but not before the thirty-seventh pair is it focused in a whole poem (page 69) with the "headland" of Lleyn alluded to in the next. This seems to mark Thomas's switch from Eglwysfach to the parish of Aberdaron in the Lleyn peninsula in 1967, where so much of the late poetry was conceived and written, and the quest received its characteristic late form. And only three poems later (page 75) the appointment with death is ominous, even if resisted:

"Not done yet" mutters
the old man, fitting a bent
poem to his broken bow.

The fortieth poem, yet there are twenty-three more to go. After service in the Aberdaron parish, Thomas's retirement in 1978 enabled him, or required him, to let temporal reminiscence imperceptibly fade. "Disproving certainties the clock knows" could thus, ironically, be said to have become Thomas's concern for the next twenty years, and we have then to ask, of *The Echoes Return Slow*, how this is autobiography, how it is soul-searching, and how poetic. It is not that these spiritual wrestlings after the fortieth poem weren't reached by much altercation between meditation and counter-meditation – Yeats's "long quarrel with himself", cited here. Rather that this process, time-located by nature, is no longer punctuated by the external incidents, acid encounters, parental deaths, awkward parishioners and rural life which still feature in the first part of *The Echoes Return Slow* and which autobiography proper would bring to us. In place of all that, is the sea's endless rhythm, summer and winter, day and night.

As said already, my own view is that biographical information should be used guardedly in evaluating poems and in responding to them. There is a fault-line between the cold fact and its metamorphosis into poetic expression which defies the detective-type reading we try to put on it. There is equally the question of how far the supposed biographical data is itself factual. Yet it would be idle to deny the strong parallels between what is offered in *The Echoes Return Slow* and what Thomas has said elsewhere, both in poetry and prose, about the events of his life. So it would be as well to list these, somewhat mechanically but in some detail, before evaluating what Thomas has made of them. In each case the left-hand ('prose') version is an albeit elliptical and attenuated rendering of what was, some time or other, a straight prose event; the right-hand version is a poem which reflects on it or takes it further imaginatively. The child was born to an English-speaking mother in Cardiff; there was some sickness. Early memories include a scrubbed doorstep and cockroaches on board his father's ship (prose pages 2-6). The child becomes boy and youth, he recalls his father's journeys at sea, and railway trains also figure. He was a fast runner, but lacked confidence, both with male fellow-students and with girls. The "building" that "towered above the town" (prose page 14) is clearly the University of Bangor.

The poet trains for the priesthood, but is more interested in birds than books. War breaks out, the freight trains go south with men and armaments. The church is not as pacifist as its founder would have wished, yet the young man fears he may be shirking a necessary courage (prose pages 16-22). Then he gets his first church appointment, in a Welsh village. His house is by the river, he notices nature, yet human questions arise in the work of the parish and he regrets having neglected his earlier studies. Agriculture adopts technology and the farmer's aim is money. Maybe a little culture, music, the arts, would be good for the parish. He visits his parishioners in their farmhouses and cottages in the evenings; he reads his books (prose pages 24-30). He marries, and is prevailed upon by his wife to have a child, their only one (a son). He sings to it in its pram, hears it cry, and maybe resents its existence (prose pages 32-38). Then comes the move from Manafon to Eglwysfach; neither is named but a shepherd's actual words are recalled: "You can almost smell the sea today". Thomas is back near the sea, as in his childhood. Cryptically the social divisions in this new parish are evoked, as is the influx of summer tourists. "The English colonise [this] parish" (prose pages 40-50).

Aspects of the poet's inner life, all also testified to in the prose work *Neb/No-one*, are alluded to in the next sections (prose 52-62). The poet walks by the sea and is attracted to certain women, meets people who like bird-watching as he does, thinks about parish life more generally and deeply. The parish youth club takes his time and attention, though he is "on the threshold of middle age" himself. Then (prose page 66) he moves up to Aberdaron in the Lleyn peninsula. He becomes deeply aware of a relation between sacrament and the elements; the pre-Cambrian rocks, the colour of sky, the deep reflections in the water, the skulls of sheep. He picks mushrooms (prose pages 64-72). His father dies (prose page 76). His own recollections now become more reflective than locally factual. We have reached the end of reminiscence and the point of changeover.

For current historicist critics the whole matter of autobiography is raised. Such readers deny that poetry is comprehensible at all except in context of the poet's life. Whatever the truth of this generally, in Wales it has added piquancy at least as a question. Thomas's voiced nationalism has often gone along with an unstinted contempt for his own people. It is hardly surprising that readers have demanded some account of it all. If Thomas's answers – with the familiar unflinching integrity – now include, for example, an apparent antipathy to his own mother and indeed to childbirth in general, then his own psychic make-up would seem to enter the equation. Thomas so long seemed to shun personal relationships outside his immediate circle, preferred rural solitude and was terse of comment generally. But as years went by, he apparently came to feel that he should give his own accounts of himself and his life, quite outside the present collection of poetry. That these were usually in Welsh (*Y Llwybrau Gynt* 1972, *Neb* 1985, *Blwyddyn yn Llŷn* 1990) is a further entangling factor. It was as though readers of Welsh alone could be trusted to read (in deeper sense) the true human subtext; as though Welsh itself, in fact, was the necessary language to convey it in, since Welsh is the tongue which has grown from the people, hills, sea coasts and then chapels and churches over the centuries, to turn back and yield its harvest now. And when finally Thomas sanctioned the publication of these autobiographies in English in 1997, it seemed that something had been laid to rest. Maybe he felt pressed to put the record straight; equally, his earthly story may just not matter any more. As *The Echoes Return Slow* has it (page 6), "there is no future but one that is safeguarded by a return to the past". Did the previous collection's timelessness suddenly seem precarious?

Surely not. The present collection is not clarified by any of this. There are several aspects of it to consider here. Far from newly uncovering a personal history, *The Echoes Return Slow* seems to assume we already know it. The sequence's first half sometimes seems like a miniature version of the dozen or so collections we have already considered. The sense of sharp memorable incidents, turning-points, aspects of the terrain, are notably similar. Being dropped (like excrement) from his mother's womb; the disconcerting birth of his own child; the ignorant peasants who yet knew the continuities of suffering; the later haughtier, more well-heeled parishioners; the empty church; the bare moorland (here it is "the woods [that] were holier than a cathedral", page 26); the wrinkled and aged in hospital; the "English" sardonically taunted; the absence of names; and the God in hiding – we don't learn any new facts nor does that seem the drive or purpose. Some poems could have come from the period of *H'm* or earlier:

> I saw the land and it was not
> waste-land, but one tilled and computed
> for harvest. And a voice, that was no
> saviour's voice, had said to the breakers:
> Be still.
> (page 29)

Some from earlier still:

> It was winter. The church shone.
> The musicians played on
> through the snow; their strings sang
> sharper than robins in the lighted interior.

From outside the white
face of the land stared in
with all the hunger of nature
in it for what it could not digest.

(page 31)

They are still fresh, still darkly beautiful (any Thomas reader knows that, to invert the proverb, *plus la meme chose, plus la change*). Of course it is more formalised, as far as it goes, as an inner life. Thomas is explicitly reflecting on himself in retrospect rather than accruing poem after poem over years which then turn out, of necessity, to have embodied his very being, his seasonal and generational progress, from the inside. Yet it might still sound like a recipe for tedium, an ageing poet's rehash of what he has long given us. That it is so much more, as it seems to me, comes from the difference between *The Echoes Return Slow* and either mere repetition or any standard "life" of the prose-autobiography sort, in the way already mentioned. It does not move to an earlier cut-off point such as Wordsworth fixed on for *The Prelude,* nor to a rounding-off with some brief and unexceptionable final comment. Rather the pastness of events merges, virtually melts, into the presentness of meditation, self-questioning and religious searching of the collection's second half. Life-reminiscence disappears as motive into something longer-term, more elusive, more lasting.

The early poem 'Here' (*Tares* 1961) had a figure for such organic change-in-continuity:

I am like a tree.
From my top boughs I can see
The footsteps that led up to me.

When the footsteps reach the top, they merge with the mind; the journey, if not complete, has redoubled on itself. The poet now questions the resulting consciousness and, typically of Thomas, the union of self, language, the past and the current state of one's deepest attitudes. The maturation of Thomas's language – the neural point at which mind, attitude and words totally disappear into each other – have turned recollection into a new mode of existence for its author. Although the yob-tourists can still reach it (and buy ice-cream and urinate/fornicate in the churchyard), "the end of a peninsula is a long way from anywhere" (page 80). The reconsideration of what is past is itself distanced from both that past and from the poems which appeared when that past was itself being lived. Having disproved the clock's certainties, Thomas enters that shadowy realm where (religious) "believing" is inseparable from both being and expressing being poetically. The matter of belief is no longer confronted by stabs and shouts and angers however frequent. Belief, whatever that means, is now inhabited.

It has many strands. Sometimes the phenomenon itself is alluded to, though always askance. It is as though the universe is empty but bugged:

> What listener
> is this, who is always awake
> and says nothing?
> (page 39)

Elsewhere the same presence is nothingness itself, closer to the Buddhist experience; elsewhere again it merges with the secular:

> Here everything happens
> far off. We exist
> on rumours, infer
> lightning from distant
>
> reports.
> (page 105)

The context is rural Wales, but Thomas has long forced the reader to take him at all levels. But this absent presence, present absence of the earlier books like *H'm* and *Frequencies*, ties in here with other aspects of the religious existence. One, clearly, is in a new aspect of Beckett-type waiting. The waiting for the absent-present to manifest itself, and the waiting for one's own death and end, become the same thing. "Not done yet" (page 75), "despite the darkness" (page 93), "ready any time now" (page 95), "it is time for bed" (page 101), "and still it goes on" (page 100), is the running-out of time that any biological creature must undergo; yet so long as consciousness remains with us, the wait for the timeless is flat, even:

> I have waited for him
>   under the tree of science,
> and he has not come
> (page 89)

But death hasn't come yet either, so the question remains open. At other times the anxieties about self which anyone shares, seem modified by these facts and presences. "Have I been brought here/to repent of my sermons?" (page103). This last might raise another timelessness, the perennial duel between love and evil. This is the spiritual and psychological universe which our consciousness inhabits and which, too, seems to elude the assertions that our experts have tried to put on it. Again and again the early prose passages in *The Echoes Return Slow*, that is to say the autobiographical ones proper, the life-events, end terse in the darkness. "The crack too narrow to squeeze through"; "rougher surfaces of the ocean"; "shelter from the storm"; "half prepared for everything but life"; "disappear into a neutral sky"; "its breast should have been his warning" (the robin); "the sapping of unanswerable questions"; "his poetry was bitter" – all these are from the first eleven pieces. And the earlier poems in the sequence too, lend a profile – not that Thomas is recording "evil" in any sinister sense. There, badness hovers from youth stunned by crass commercialism ("up in the hills they looked at one another appalled and turned on the transistors", page 64) to "no cure for old age" (page 62 – a curious inversion of chronological time). But more widely the daily human condition, in which we live with our genetic and evolutionary inheritance, and struggle for food, warmth and companionship or their dangerous excesses, brings on evil both intended and unintended; the car crash and the thalidomide child, but the Idi Amin and the Fred West too (my own examples), not to mention the mushroom–shaped cloud (page 74) either. The scientist and civic officer properly seek earthly amelioration, but the haunted soul dwells within the permanent contradiction. It is hard to keep faith with evil's opposite, love, but only because love's very nature is self-effacing; "love stands, renouncing itself" (page 117). In fact Thomas's very latest years, as it were beyond the strife, seem to have taken this struggle mainly down to his own self-denying, perhaps self-despising condition. Seeing old ladies in hospital beds ("blonde dolls, their joints twisted", page 63) recalls "earth's huge draughts/of joy and woe", but this is a rarer summary. Rather, and here the prose-autobiographical evidence is not avoidable, we think of Neb, "Nobody", as Thomas takes himself to be. It is between the poles of the child who thought of himself as excrement and the man who evaporates into the divine nullity of the entire cosmos. For secular humans evil destroys God's existence, but for the haunted religious evil gives it a character that can never depart.

These and other angles on eternity are increasingly couched in the language that has now been honed for some sixty years to express them. In literary terms this is metaphor and irony. Thomas's familiar metaphoric resource is still evident. Eichmann "played on his/victims' limbs the symphony/of perdition" (page 23), and Thomas like a maths teacher puts a "cross" (i.e. crucifixion too) at the bottom of people's problem-answers "to prove to them that they were wrong" (page 89). Yet more deeply metaphor, and linguistic turn of every kind, now so saturate the work that the straight statements are exceptional. When the poet lied "about his ability to play Bridge" (page 52), the socialising parishioners he was addressing reminded him of "officers' mess, receptions"; I for one can't avoid recalling the mariner father and the "bridge" where the captain stood in command of his vessel. Every poem here and every prose piece is by now such a network of criss-cross references, allusions, double-meanings and half-meanings – it is now so ingrained in the poet's vocation and existence – that any idea of a "statement" about "belief" seems redundant.

All this has, of course, been earned over a lifetime's work. But it also amounts to a demand, by the poet, that it too is metaphysical and cosmic. The lines cited earlier, "Have I been brought here/to repent of my sermons?" feel like metaphor but are drawn from the ground of all metaphor in the pluralities of reality. Language is itself a product of evolved brain and obdurate matter, the actual capacity of mineral and plant to yield ink and paper in signal form. The ancient "word of God", as was seen earlier, is language itself; and in these final collections Thomas's total immersion for so long in this possibility leads to the saturation already suggested. Wallace Stevens once said that he had become chary of taking poetic snapshots, i.e. metaphors too clear-cut. I don't know whether Thomas took this aboard specifically but he has often acknowledged his debt to the American poet.

Watery figures of immersion and saturation of course point again to the sea, the pervading trope in *The Echoes Return Slow*. Not now the rare sea bird of 'Sea-watching' (*Laboratories of the Spirit*) but the sea itself, in its indistinction and boundlessness. It is beyond the horizon and in the unreachable depths, and serves as link between earthly finitude and the unknowable:

> I lie
> in the lean hours awake, listening
> to the swell born somewhere in the Atlantic
> rising and falling, rising and falling,
> wave on wave on the long shore
> by the village, that is without light
> and companionless. And the thought comes
> of that other being who is awake, too,
> letting our prayers break on him
> not like this for a few hours,
> but for days, years, for eternity.
>
> (page 79)

The sea comes inland when a shepherd smells it. Thomas both sniffs and hears it by the shore; the headland juts out into it as though time reached the timeless. Fish approach him vacantly and then recede into the depths; seaweed sways like "Salome dancing before a salt throne". The bedridden women "keep afloat over bottomless fathoms", and flowers from funerals are "flotsam cast up by the perennial tide". The poet is "ready any time now/for walking the bone's/plank over the dark waters". But all the while, the sea's changes point up the limits of our own. It "revises itself over and over. When he arose in the morning or looked at it at night, it was always at a new version of it" (page 102). This last is in context of the priest's poor opinion of Prayer Book revisions. To extract these examples is, of course, itself to put them in small bottles while the oceans go on overwhelming us in their huger indivisibilities. The wider comparison, or actual experience, of the sea is to find the poet ever restless in both time and space; and this itself is a last comment on belief.

This belief is ironic; indeed it is a perpetual state of irony. Thomas's lifelong terseness, as said already, appears in the word that means two things so unobtrusively that language and existence themselves seem permanently implicated. So, finally, there is no "belief" – or disbelief, or even doubt – in plain prose; just two responses. One is the "Amen" that fleetingly surfaces in sundry places (pages 45, 56, 103 and 117) and which we have seen before. Not "Credo" but "Amen"; not "I believe" but "So be it", the acceptance of the presence that always eludes, always remains. Then learning to respond to that too, Thomas turns back to his peasants:

                   There were depths
         in some of them I shrank back
         from, wells that the word 'God'
         fell into and died away,
         and for all I know is still
         falling.

                        (page 25)

Thomas himself had dropped the stone into the well's depths in previous poems; the listening means a long silence before the answer
that defers answer or is no answer. The echoes return slow.

Counterpoint (1990) has a new structure of its own. It has four
parts, 'B.C.', 'Incarnation', 'Crucifixion' and 'A.D.'. As in the previous collection the poems have no titles. But here they are separate
poems entirely; they work round the named themes although they
are hardly a "sequence" as that is usually understood. These historical stages are barely marked by the events of history's diary. It is
more a matter of the Old Testament, the start and end of the story
of Christ, and then ideas from many eras down to science now;
these, however, do not observe any strict chronology. The book is
Thomas's most exclusively religious yet, for unlike its predecessor
The Echoes Return Slow it comes from nowhere; and unlike even
Laboratories of the Spirit there is no discernible landscape of home or
country. This may be the "counterpoint" of the title, a reference to
the autobiographical setting the previous book had started to work
away from.

Rather *Counterpoint* begins at prehistory. It is a terrain of sorts,
but the first theme is utterance itself. In the same way, for anthro-
pologists, language is where homo sapiens is first to be identified.
The book's very first line, "This page should be left blank", has the
wintry Thomas hallmark. But it turns out literal: "snow where the
abominable footprints/have not yet appeared", though the one
double meaning is not resisted. Certainly the snow feels real here, or
at least a symbol of the harsh conditions our first ancestors had to
cope with. But the rupture at language's heart is given mythically:

         No, in the beginning was silence
         that was broken by the word
         forbidding it to be broken.
                        (page 9)

Writing and speech, sight and sound, entangled from the start as to which has priority; but the paradox too, that to forbid communication is itself a communication. Terrain returns with the garden of Eden, but again to subvert a myth; "Of course there was no serpent" (page 11). In substituting the mirror for the woman's tempter, Thomas eases the first story for some purpose hard to fathom; and when writing of the Christ-child he superimposes the later over the earlier:

> This is Eden
> over again. The child
> holds out both his hands
> for the breast's apple. The snake is asleep.
>
> (page 28)

The poem ends there. In between, Jacob and Bethel are touched on, but the pre-Christian story is rendered, insofar as it is at all, in terms of myth given in shavings, snatches, glimpses, all re-turned and interpreted. "How could they know, the first farmers,/the sowing of corn was the sowing of armed men?" (page 16). In the third section furthermore, 'A.D.', there are few references before the twentieth century, and one of them is dismissive, if ironically so:

> Forget it. The Middle Ages
> are over. On a bone
> altar, with radiation
> for candle, we make sacrifice
> to the god of quasars
> and pulsars, wiping
> our robotic hands clean
> on a disposable conscience.
>
> (page 49)

('Quasars' sic.) And in between, the two sections on Christ omit his life entirely. There is no parable, no miracle, no disciples. From his cradle the child goes straight to his death on the cross. In two poems (pages 24, 29) the two events appear together. Now it seems then, that whatever conscious aim Thomas had in writing this collection – and my guess rather is that the arrangement evolved gradually – there is really a threefold absorption with myth, man and science. There is the myth of the world's beginning, Christ as prototype of man's known suffering, and science as myth's replacement and final destroyer. Behind this trinity is the elusive entity never far away – variously it, he, God – which these other three entities try to evoke, avoid or appease.

But in a short but key poem Thomas suggests, I think, that science too is myth. This of course doesn't discredit science as far as it goes, indeed it reminds us of the truth-basis that any myth must have to exert power over us. This applies even if that "truth" is not a sort we are used to or can use in daily life. But here is the poem (page 56):

> They will come to understand
> our folk-tale was the machine.
> We listened to it in the twilight
> of our reason, taking it as the hour
>
> in which truth dawned. They will return
> without moving to an innocence
> as in advance of their knowledge
> as the smile of the Christ child was of its cross.

That is to say, when we inhabit a myth we can make it work; it isn't baseless; but it is only "true" so far as it goes. The poem posits a future society looking back at our own. Just as the medieval myth of necessary static society (feudalism) disappeared with the expansion of trading and money, so the myth that science can solve all practical problems may disappear as these problems, rather, seem under science exponentially to increase. The demand for energy burns up the planet while increased medical skill crowds it to bursting point.

In risking this large adaptation, Thomas may be revealing how his creative mind has always worked in dealing with more local areas. For again and again he transposes the terms of a known fact, or a standard metaphor, into a striking new arrangement. Early in *Counterpoint* the magi's gifts of gold, frankincense and myrrh become "gifts of heart, mind and soul". He re-uses the Eden tree too, for he "climbed into/the tree of knowledge/of good and evil to add/to my stature" (pages 24, 17). Yeats is in his tower "poring over the manuscript/of his people" (page 57) ; i.e. the figure in Yeats's tower poems ('Ego Dominus Tuus' and 'The Phases of the Moon' most obviously) pores over his book, and Thomas directs this outward to Ireland. This has been a Thomas touch for a long time. God "put his hand in his side" in *Frequencies* and earlier; the believer rather than the saviour is nailed to the tree; the cross is the pylon (in *Counterpoint* the gantry); the stones of adultery are hurled at different targets.

The tendency might be expected to grow further, under this general umbrella and auspices of myth itself gone creative, with a poet who uses and re-uses the same host of tropes again and again over the decades of his work. We've summarized them before, but the list grows. The scientist's dissections. The bone. The gene. The virus. The black hole. The receding god. The machine. The glass and the mirror. The breaking of bread and of the wave. The tree. The equation. The woman's hair. The empty church. The bird. The lens. The knife. The galaxy. The night sky. Radar. Aircraft. The serpent. The moon. The well. The burning bush. The flower. The bare moor. In the earliest periods there was also the priest, the shadow and the altar, the shepherd and the sheep, and the humble cottage and fireside.

But as good R.S. Thomas readers, by now we ought surely to have heard the sly tempter at least once whispering to us. Is it all suddenly baseless? *Counterpoint* has the religious yearning of *Frequencies* and *Laboratories of the Spirit*, but there is less formality, less general expansion; it comes and is gone; it is clipped. Maybe Thomas is running these poems off now by an easy formula, a mere technique. Maybe these are the last shreds of worn-out symbols. He certainly has the skill and talent and, from the list just given, apparently the inventory of materials. Worse still then; is the old man going ga-ga, "foaming poetry at the mouth" as he puts it himself (page 60), mechanically trying every arrangement of terms in order, no longer to approach God (he is as drawn to Buddhism now, he tells us) but just to keep himself occupied and the flag of his reputation flying? At times – rarely – he is even banal, we might feel: "Lord of the molecule and the atom/are you Lord of the gene too?" Or of the dance.

It might seem this is what all this playing and replaying of the supposed "absent god" amounts to, both here and in previous books. It is a chance to deploy every combination of his figures, metaphors, symbols and word-skills, all in the name of what turns out to be a bogus theology and predictably so. For if language is so important, then a language-conjurer – and there's a bit about conjuring and the jester here and there – could keep the circle of variations going easily enough and allude to the empty centre every so often with just enough mystification to keep his loyal readers happy. I don't suggest all such would be deliberate, less still deliberately deceitful. But the ever-growing oeuvre must take the reader into new itches and enticements. More and more do you want to put one meaning beside another, the image beside its first appearance twenty or thirty years earlier, the poem beside the earlier poem and both beside the man himself. You want to rank double-entendre from straight pun down to imperceptible mergers of nuance where we hardly know which meaning to place as notionally first. Thomas's capacity to keep ahead of his public is alluded to time and again by admiring critics and reviewers. The movement of *Counterpoint* lies, again, in each poem moving away from the one before; by catching us unawares, by a clear reversal, by new tropes or figures, or by simply changing the subject. More than once the present writer was thinking "but what about – ?", only to find the next poem allayed the matter. Yet even so, all this may serve the poet more severely, you might say, now he has gone, the work wound up, and readers in the years ahead see it in a different order, from a finished perspective.

I just don't believe it. Certainly there are some familiar set-pieces, some list-poems, and some tours-de-force. But many poems still test the sinew; they suggest that the struggle with the furies was not over. We couldn't show this without a thorough account of several poems, but here are two which may stand in for the others enough to make the point.

> There is a being, they say,
> neither body nor spirit,
> that is more power than reason, more reason
> than love, whose origins
> are unknown, who is apart
> and with us, the silence
> to which we appeal, the architect
> of our failure. It takes the genes
> and experiments with them and our children
> are born blind, or seeing have
> smooth hands that are the instruments
> of destruction. It is the spoor
> in the world's dark leading away
> from the discovered victim, the expression
> the sky shows us after

an excess of spleen. It has gifts it
distributes to those least fitted
to use them. It is everywhere and
nowhere, and looks sideways into the shocked face
of life, challenging it to disown it.

(page 20)

Counterpoint contains a few poems in this mode (pages 33, 34, 48), taut rhythmic renderings of thought pushed through down the spines of their main and conditional phrases. The most wonderful it would seem is near the end (page 61), "The imperatives of the instincts", as tight and full as any in these later collections. Although "There is a being" is a list-poem syntactically, each consideration belongs within the one intellectual rhythm where the poet seeks truth most; and the result is a balance morally and metaphysically. On the face of it the "being" is on the bad side, but such writing doesn't allow that easy division. That it is "more power than reason, more reason/than love" doesn't seem to rule love out, rather it quietly includes it. Equally that it is "apart/and with us, the silence/to which we appeal" seems to leave it accessible, not wholly beyond that appeal. The "architect" of failure leaves us uneasy yet calmed at once. Something, it seems, is in order. The evil we suffer comes only from "experiments", not from cruelty, destructiveness or malice. That it distributes "gifts" doesn't seem entirely ironic this time, and the Darwinian "fitted" works both ways. Either Darwinian survival is refuted, suggesting science is not so reliable in its belief in cut-throat competition's success; or the phrase is gentler altogether. The world's poor – in riches or biological endowment – get a share after all; the last shall be first and the first shall be last. And finally, we swing back to the opening line anyway; "there is a being, *they* say," (my emphasis); maybe this is one more rumour to distract us from truth itself.

The typical Thomas tropes – architect, genes, blind children, spoor, excess of spleen, gifts – though not all firsts here, are hardly merely re-runs. The characteristic suppleness of the long phrases' tail-ends show a thought unwinding; the poem has only five sentences. A rather different poem, more one we might have felt suspicious of, is this (page 29):

The Nativity? No.
Something has gone wrong.

There is a hole in the stable
acid rain drips through
onto an absence. Beauty
is hoisted upside down.
The truth is Pilate not
lingering for an answer.
The angels are prostrate
"beaten into the clay"
as Yeats thundered. Only
Satan beams down,
poisoning with fertilizers
the place where the child
lay, harrowing the ground
for the drumming of the machine-
gun tears of the rich that are
seed of the next war.

"No" and "wrong" avoid any over-theological "evil" by thudding
down the first two line-ends sharply. The "hole" in the roof, for the
Thomas reader, links with the cosmic black holes he so often alludes
to, and this can be done because his terms are seldom slapdash,
always precise. The inverted flag on the mast (beauty hoisted upside
down) might come from Thomas's mariner stock though one can
hardly be sure. The switch from an old motif to a new one, alluded
to above, finds Pilate, like Oedipus, himself the answer to his own
question. When Satan "beams" down it is smile and radiation at
once, and the "poison" of the next line is both the chemical that kills
the pest and the venom of the serpent, the first pest itself. "Harrow",
"seed"; more weight of meaning is added. By the end we sense, or I
sense, that this marshalling of one-off poetic observations has worked
as a continued utterance, held in place by its truncated lines and
spare rhythm. There are numerous pieces like this in this collection,
and most work, at minimum, to link the solider or longer utterances.

And there are some brilliant plays on words (for example the last
line of 'B.C.', page 34) and some notable new metaphors, including
the "concrete and macadam/that are the lava/pouring from the erup-
tion/of the species". More generally though Thomas's metaphors are
no longer the full-blown creations of earlier years. Yet this seems
intentional. The poetry's syntaxes seem more fitting repositories of
any attempt to express the unknowable, its invisible shape and pressure. Thomas is resisting the Beckettian descent into lessness, the

place where language would say and be nothing at all. In just two places (pages 18, and 29's title) language collapses. Thomas overdoes the rhetorical questions maybe, but in one's eighties "after the Amens fade" there could be a drain on what there is left to state. Occasionally poems state a position and a moral, even a reprimand (pages 37, 42). Perhaps the need to keep ahead is born of his own dissatisfaction.

We open the next book, *Mass for Hard Times* (1992), wondering what on earth was left to follow the supposed autobiography and the relentless search, this time historical, for that ever-elusive centre behind creation itself. But what we find, is a surprising swing toward order. Ostensibly at least, *Mass for Hard Times* contains far more poems than before of strong external architecture. The opening sequence, the title poem, has five sections, 'Kyrie', 'Gloria', 'Credo', 'Sanctus' and 'Benedictus'. But in three of these the respective stanzas are uniform, liturgical; each is a variant on the exact formula:

> From the body at its meal's end
> and its messmate whose meal is beginning,
> > > Gloria.

> From the early and late cloud, beautiful and deadly
> as the mushroom we are forbidden to eat,
> > > Gloria.

> From the stars that are but as dew
> and the viruses outnumbering the star clusters,
> > > Gloria.

> From those waiting at the foot of the helix
> for the rope-trick performer to come down,
> > > Gloria.

And so on. Ironic but far from negative, any search or question is in abeyance. As the poet puts it elsewhere ('Sonata in X') he is now not always on his knees but sometimes "perpendicular". The poems throughout have titles. Their variety is great – more so indeed than in many earlier collections – but it seems more than usually arranged round the poems of edifice.

The second such poem, 'The God', underlines the point. The God turns out to have five clear aspects, a veritable pentagon. There is the god of poets, musicians, artists, scientists and theologians; these too are section titles. A sixth section, 'Who Is', gives us the god "whose mind/is its own fountain, who/overflows". Again then this god is not now desperately sought but confidently affirmed. Comparable poems are 'Match My Moments', a series of recalled incidents poignant or imaginative. The phrase "that time", which leads each one in, establishes a parity they must be scrutinized under. Another poem 'Markers' gives five of its six regular stanzas each to a philosopher, the names of four of them being the lead-in word for each. In 'Monday's Child' each stanza is labelled by a day of the week. Naturally then 'The Seasons' has four labelled sections. Of course my summary makes it all seem more mechanical than it is. But the collection as a whole seems able to look out from the upper windows of these buildings to a wider and in part recognizably earthly landscape. There are many of the shorter pieces of inner and outer probing we expect from their author, but it is as though they too are now part of that landscape, lying there alongside fauna, people, water, and bits of Wales.

Three other poems are just as structured, and extend up to five pages each, but in a different way. These are 'R.I.P.', 'Bleak Liturgies' and 'Sonata in X', the final poem whose size and spread is thus in equilibrium with the book's beginning. These poems are less exactly symmetrical. Rather they are made up of a mixture of shorter pieces, a method we haven't seen since *Later Poems* and before that 'Border Blues' right at the start of *Poetry for Supper* over thirty years earlier. These separate sections could be – may well have first been – separate poems, but their gathering into single works is more than convenience. Thomas's poems have long been seen to be the life-continuum which in other poets might have resulted in a longer single work.

In asking what we make of these new structurings one might first notice how much the first two of these three poems hang round a single topic: language. It is a slippery topic, and too easy a resort for the critic; but yet more analyses of metaphors and syntax is not the point here. Rather, Thomas seems to have come to yet another new conclusion about language, and it is tied very deeply to the standing off, in this book, from the seemingly endless search for the god-vacated presence of earlier books.

'R.I.P.' with its epigraph '1588-1988' is about the sixteenth century clergyman William Morgan, vicar of Llanrhaeadr-ym

Mochnant, who translated the Bible into Welsh. This mattered much to Thomas, hardly surprisingly, and he had already produced a poem on the subject ('Llanrhaeadr ym Mochnant') over twenty years before in *Not That He Brought Flowers*. Morgan's work had incalculable influence, not only on the church in Wales but on Welsh education and poetry, and the consolidation of the language as vehicle of Welsh culture (rather than only speech) at a time when the Welsh gentry were strongly disposed to identify with English and the court. Oversimplifying, it was agreed by the English administration and by all parties in Wales, that English should be the language of bureaucracy and Welsh of religion.

At least some historians believe that loyalty to the religion was what was at stake, and that the English were more concerned to secure a Protestant Wales than an English-reading one. There is some irony in the date of publication (1588), that of the defeat of the Spanish Armada, and some see Morgan's dedication to the Queen and Archbishop Whitgift as sycophantic. However, Whitgift supported the project wholeheartedly, expediting its completion and probably footing much of the bill.

The interested reader is referred to John Davies's excellent account (see Bibliography) for more detail, much of it germane to Thomas's poem and its place in *Mass for Hard Times*. Thomas starts with the expected scepticism:

> And the Englishman asks:
> How do you say it? Twitching
> his nostril at the odiousness
> of comparisons between a Welsh
> village and capital of the world
> as instruments of salvation.

For Thomas, Whitgift's seeming generosity was because "the book was to be used/for the promotion of English". The translation was made both in Llanrhaedr-ym-Mochnant and London. But Thomas has already given a remarkable and appealing description of Morgan working away, searching for the right word much like an angler (shades of Isaac Walton perhaps) hanging over a river:

> ...his mind's fly time
> and again on its surface,
> angling for the right word...

> Imagine his delight
> in striking those Welsh nouns,
>
> as they rose from the shadows,
> that are as alive as ever,
> stippling the book's page.

Thomas's championing of Welsh is not in question. Yet through the power of his own image he may also have moved to a sense of how it is with any language whatsoever:

> Is an obsession with language
> an acknowledgement we are too late
> to save it?

"Language", not "the language". At my quick count the word "language" appears in the book thirteen times. But more to the point is "vocabulary", six times and not previously appearing, as I recall, in the Thomas oeuvre, even though as he says "We have been victims/of vocabulary for too long" ('Question'). "Literature", "grammar", "dictionary" and "translation", once each, add to the impression of a shift of emphasis. It is there too in a key stanza from 'The Letter':

> I look up from my book,
> from the unreality of language,
> and stare at the sea's surface
> that says nothing and means it.

Since Thomas continued to write poetry, more and more indeed it seems as he aged, language's "unreality" is likely to mean something not negative but specific. The American linguist Joseph Graham has said that "words do not take the place of thoughts. They occupy a different place". Words defer themselves, add end on, go ever to the right. They move across the terrain to one hearing them, or to the objects, trees, horizon, buildings, from which they rebound to us. And they make formal liturgies. There are several allusions, in *Mass for Hard Times*, to language's material provenance, its self-reference. It is, in no reprehensible sense, like the sea a thing of surface. Again one thinks of Thomas's repeatedly acknowledged debt to Wallace Stevens, the American poet of surface as more than depth, as the only place where anything's nature can be really witnessed. If we slice a thing's surface off it, to see what is beneath, that deeper layer itself becomes the surface, itself the new receptor of light. We saw an earlier interest in surface in the poems on French Impressionism in *Between Here and Now*. What then is the point, Thomas now seems to have asked himself, of my continuing to address this non-surface, deep, hidden thing, the he, it or god which refuses to answer, or whose very answer is silence? Haven't I now done that to exhaustion? Thomas recalls the Eastern religions' injunctions that the sacred name should never be uttered: "Behind the word is the name/not to be known for fear/we should gain power over it" ('The Reason'). To cease that probe does not mean one has stopped believing in its target's existence. Rather, the poet simply raises his head to the different matter of expressing the godhead, whatever that is, on this earth and now: in short, the liturgies of the church and the translations of the Bible. As the New Age writer Ken Wilber might have put it, there is less depth, more span. Language doesn't dive down to the heart searching for an absence-presence; it spreads sideways like seeping water across all the space available to it. Much of the book, always serious, is decidedly good-humoured; for example 'Credo' in the title-poem itself. 'Bleak Liturgies', another long poem, is a more general concern about the state of ecclesiastical language in the modern era, in a church ravaged not only by media but by transport, design, cacophony and much else. Concrete is everywhere, missionaries arrive by jet, crucifixes are mass produced to hang round the necks of punks. From a 1998 perspective Thomas was not just topical but prophetic: "re-editing the scriptures/we come on a verse suggesting/that we be gay, so gay we are".

It isn't clear, and probably does not matter, whether this new attitude to language led to the book's wider interests or derived from them. It is shorter on obsession and longer on survey. I wouldn't want to be misunderstood here. "Word" remains prevalent along with "language", "vocabulary" and the rest. 'The Reason' is one of Thomas's profoundest meditative poems. Some poems, like 'Tell Us' and 'Could Be', address the present-absent God as edgily and uncertainly as ever. But rather more, like 'Tidal' and 'Eschatology', make that entity third person and see the probe as itself a project to be examined detachedly, its work temporarily done. Instead, a continuum of poems goes from those first probes through to ones that look at the world, locally and more widely, to see where religion is, or earthly life.

There is a poem about a moth; and one on newts:

> In a pool
> on the mountain
> newts live, semi-
> palmated, grey-faced
> as stone; reptilian
> gargoyles on cornices
> of water. Their world
> stretches from horizon
> to horizon, which is
> two feet by two.
>
>   Here
> everything happens:
> pain, bliss, hunger –
> but what are a newt's
> thoughts? Their brows corrugated
> from long pondering
> a scaled truth they rest
> panting like life itself
> on the wondering journey
> that is without end.
>   ('Newts')

There is the same imagery of buildings and horizons; but the interest in the newt's thoughts shows a long-term absorption in evolution's stages themselves, and Thomas's now two-decade battle with contemporary science. The precise, careful observation of the newt argues that a humanistic or poetic engagement with the lower-kingdom world may be as fertile as that of the bio-geneticist. "Pondering" is more than just a pun; it conveys exactly that to a newt, thought and pond-existence may be identical. In this apparently new phase, of faith that God's absence is in God's purview not ours, "science" is as likely to mean "scientist". One suspects that writers like Peter Atkins, Richard Dawkins and Stephen Jay Gould have been part of Thomas's reading, along with the more sympathetically disposed (religion-wise) Paul Davies; yet all of us are now "Mobile man, wheeled man,/man trying to keep up/with himself" ('The Refusal'). But it is the scientists who must pray "upside-down in their space chambers" ('What Then?'), who is "immaculately dressed not /conceived" ('Eschatology'), and who, Narcissus-like ignoring the voice of his love Echo:

> still bends
> over his cloning, call as she may,
> irrefutable beside the gene-pool.
>
> ('Hark')

Fair or not, thanks to the double-meaning the picture is of the scientist, too, out in field and moorland as well as in laboratory. Water as either mirror or transparent glass, depending how we look at them, goes back to Wordsworth and Herbert, both poets of the palpable world for all their different visionary perspectives.

And Wales gently shimmers back into the poems, after the more existential absorptions of *Counterpoint*. But even while the politics still hover, as in 'R.I.P. 1588-1988', it is a Wales one inhabits, it is local. Fish, newts, moths, nectar and bracken are parts of a wider yet still small acreage. 'Plas-yn-Rhiw' (hill house; where the Thomases lived in Lleyn before he moved to Anglesey) has little left for the poet. But this may be because his wife's death left him lonely — Mildred Eldridge is the collection's dedicatee — and the moss and flowers of his garden sit easily enough about him still. 'Afon Rhiw', hill stream, plays its metaphoric depths, but with a remarkable turnabout. The fish looks up at the poet himself:

> Questioned, the trout had confessed
> I was indistinguishable
> from a tree, roots in darkness
> my head in the clouds, and that like
> thoughts, too, their best place
> was among the shadows rather
> than being drawn into the light's
> dryness to perish of too much air.

Yet the poet doesn't really have his "head in the clouds" in the colloquial sense, that is to say absentmindedly; he is right there fishing. 'Aside', 'Winter', 'Seasons' and other poems make the natural world of garden, ploughland and wood visible from the perpendicular stance, man erect again. The new mood is conveyed with relaxed control in 'Retired', one of the collections' key poems:

> Not to worry myself any more
> if I am out of step, fallen behind.

> Let the space probes continue;
> I have a different distance to travel.

"Distance" not "road", for

> Here I can watch the night sky,
> listen to how one grass blade
> grates on another as member
> of a disdained orchestra.

The fullness and easement of language, after the exclusive wrestling of other recent books for "something I was near and never attained", yields its crop of new tropes. (Certainly no danger then, of the same few ever circling each other.) The mushroom is characteristically edible on the ground but a huge poison that drops fall-out from the air. The knee appears, but no longer only for prayer. God is "the ventriloquist/who once sat Christ/on your knee" ('Could Be'), and growing up means giving up "the burying of the head/between God's knees" ('One Life'), another angle on the book's new departure from obsession. Entirely new one-off metaphors appear, themselves often of edifice. The Christian message has been obscured by "the furniture departments/of our churches", and the poet finds himself "pulling thought's buildings/down to make way for new". Sexuality brings some captivating double-play, "breasts/risen to his first kneading", while within the girl in the wheatfield "palpitating,/was the heart's poppy". Thomas's own wordplay is subject of a strong comparison:

> the word like a sword
> turning both ways
> to keep the gates of vocabulary.
>   ('The God')

The chief change in the collection, though, is the diversifying of the Christian cross as a rich symbol. It is still "untenanted", suggesting maybe that not just Christ but any human may expect to have to bear it, or climb on it, at life's darkest moments. But twice it is now a signpost on the road, pointing both ways, and it is beneficent:

> to erect the Calvary
> that is our signpost, arms

> pointing in opposite directions
> to bring us in the end
>
> to the same place, so impossible
> is it to escape love.
>   ('The Word')

This hasn't appeared before. The cross turned up quite often in *Counterpoint* but not yet as a rich image. In earlier books it had usually been the tree, the cross still in natural state. In *Mass for Hard Times* the signpost idea also appears in the title poem, a little differently in that it is merely "pointing both ways", implying opportunity or dilemma. That Thomas uses this twice suggests that he has been newly drawn to its metaphoric potential. For in the title-poem it is the crossbow, "The Cross, that long-bow drawn against love". Later that image is developed. "The cross/is an old-fashioned/weapon, but its bow/is drawn unerringly/against the heart" ('Sure'). In 'Retired' it is struck by the lightning of Christ's body. In 'The God' it is an aircraft or rocket for humanity to fly on. Characteristically of this book too, the symbol spreads outwards; the signpost can also come without the cross, entailing the poet's medium itself:

> Wittgenstein's signposts pointing
> at the boundaries of language
> into the obligatory void.
>   ('Markers')

And when the cross has the scarecrow on it, that image comes first; that is to say, the symbol is merged with its surroundings and drawn out from them:

>   Of whom
> does the scarecrow remind
> arms wide as though pierced
>
> by the rain's nails, while
> the motorist goes by insolently
> wagging his speedometer's finger?
>   ('Come Down')

The key to the cross's diversification is stated clearly in 'What Then?' "You chose the natural timber/to die on that the natural/man should be saved". But this naturalness now refers less to the "tree", Thomas's usual comparison in earlier years. The cross is now arte- fact. Cultivated in the natural world, it is a made object of wood, and so tied to humanity, homo faber but equally earthborn. It is as though the absence of the absent god can no longer be tolerated, and Thomas is back with a more orthodox Christianity. Now, like David Jones, he sees incarnation as divinity in all the processes of living; his house, village and local trout stream , scarecrows in the fields, hills in the distance, rocks on the shore, weeds in the garden, political Wales, books and buildings and windows and furniture and language.

And finally, love seems to come more easily. This poet, so often charged with bilious contempt for the tasteless and aggression toward political or class opponents, now expresses the love that emerges from lack of strain, in natural surroundings in the calm of retirement. It is fullest in 'A Marriage'. This is an already much- cherished poem by Thomas's readers, for its testimony to his wife, in a moment the more moving for its indirection and soft under- statement:

> "Come" said death,
> choosing her as his
>   partner for
> the last dance. And she,
>   who in life
> had done everything
>   with a bird's grace,
> opened her bill now
>   for the shedding
> of one sigh no
>   heavier than a feather.

No Truce with the Furies, Thomas's final collection published in his lifetime, contains a poem which in other circumstances might well have followed 'A Marriage':

> That day after the night death;
> that night after the day's wailing,
> I went out on the hill
> and contemplated the lit windows
> and the stars, those flocks
> without a shepherd; and I asked:

"Is she up there, the woman
who was the pawn that love
offered in exchange for beauty?"

Later I was alone in my room
reading and, the door closed,
she was there, speechlessly enquiring:
Was all well? It was true
what the book said in answer
to the world's question as to where
at death does the soul go:
"There is no need under a pillarless
heaven for it to go anywhere."

('The Morrow')

The poem was presumably written after Elsi's death, possibly just
before it. Either way there is some finality; a bridge is crossed. The
male needs to know where she is; the female needs to know if he is
all right. The "book" reassures; it doesn't assert that the soul goes
nowhere, less still that it ceases to exist. It says more calmly that the
question should not fret us. If this poem is symptomatic of the collection, it implies that the best response to the restless questioning
of earlier years was to accept that all answers are tentative by their
nature.

The onus is therefore thrown on to how both questions and
"answers" are expressed. It is their framing at all that we are per-
mitted by earthly existence. Other poems in the collection, though
not for the first time, touch the matter generally:

Christmas; the themes are exhausted.
Yet there is always room
on the heart for another
snowflake to reveal a pattern.

('Blind Noel')

The habit of writing supervenes any chance that there is nothing left
to say; yet this is not necessarily negative. The last three lines can
as well be read straight as sardonically. More to the point is that the
tiniest nuance, merely "another snowflake" in a white landscape,
may still add something. The same idea ends a poem of that name,
'Nuance':

                    To pray, perhaps, is
        to have a part in an infinitesimal deflection.

Other poems wonder whether language is the only means of communication:

> What do the whales say
> calling to one another
> on their extended wave-lengths?
> Why suppose that it is language?
> It is pain searching for
> an echo. It is regret
> for a world that has men
> in it.
>   ('No Jonahs')

In 'Near and Far' the matter is expanded further but differently (the
present/absent godhead is addressed as so often):

> You have no words yet vibrate
> in me with the resonance of an Amen...
> but always as far off
> as you are near, terrifying
> me as much by your proximity
> as by your being light-years away.

That is to say, the elusive being never answers yet always commu-
nicates in its own mode; and it occupies no one spot yet only feels
absent by being so dispersed across reality as to be invisible to
mortal near-sightedness.

All this says something about this collection's status. Although it
is the final one, there may presumably be other poems in the bottom
drawer which become available at some later date. (There are certainly published but uncollected poems around in various magazines.)
Yet it is difficult to read it as other than final. Perhaps more than usually with R.S. Thomas, this collection adds little in the way of any
obvious new thrust forward. All the more remarkable that the poems
still engage us, still come up with some new turn of phrase, aspect of
the infinite, or science, or early sexuality, which we have not had
before. It suggests that he never wrote a poem unless the pressure was
there to do so. Yet the mix is now fully familiar. And as I have tried
to suggest, it seems self-knowingly so. Something near to a recogni-

tion has been achieved, that the endless search for expression of the godhead is itself that expression, no less and no more.

One might at last then try to summarize Thomas's theology, insofar as that can be gleaned from the glimpses, metaphors, probings, demands and the rest over the many years. Unsurprisingly – though it usually less explicit – it is T.S. Eliot rather than Stevens or Yeats who lurks, in part, behind this theme in Thomas, even while the total problem is always Thomas's own. God (so to name it) cannot be named, because that would include such in our language. God is not contravened by science yet is always a step ahead of science. God entails rather than is entailed by pain, and that often feels destructive; yet somehow it is more worthwhile than that in the last analysis, even though it is not given to us to understand. Insofar as God is creator, the creation is of a rich substance, "matter" certainly but a material which can be rendered into symbol by its very essence; water, bone, tree, atom, virus, galaxy and the rest. This is 'nature', which we tamper with at risk. God elicits a kind of pleading from mortals, called prayer, whether for sustenance or information; this prayer isn't "answered" in any obvious way but is still meaningful and in some wider sense not ignored. Meanwhile there is a kind of apparatus around on earth, in the form of church, book, chalice, liturgy and the rest, not God-made but still authentic in that it is a response from limited individuals to all these half-sensed features of God as such. At the heart is love, quite uncompromisingly so; but it is idle to expect it overtly at every corner, or indeed more than seldom. Love is hard-won in this universe, it seems, and the loving God intends such a state of affairs, in a way that Thomas sometimes regards as contrary if not perverse. Like the birds of prey, God is raptor (frequently in *No Truce with the Furies* though seldom directly), but the seizure is of something valued by the predator for its best nature. If God is raptor, man is rapt. It is love, but a ferocious love.

One must ask then whether the poet "believes" all this. I sense that this too may have troubled readers who think of belief as confidence placed in doctrinal statements. The sort of Thomas-critic who opens by saying, "of course, I'm not a believer myself", then renders belief down to assent to a piddling assertion. One loses confidence that they understand the position at all. To "believe in God", Thomas implies on every page (no less so in the latest collection), is to know that such belief is arduous and oscillating, that

God has it so, that God stands aside while evil makes such belief an agony, and that to "believe" is itself a stressed state by its nature; yet finally that all this is done for a love we can barely comprehend or note. Such a package is torment and reward at once, in precarious balance; neither gives ground to the other. But this puts language itself to the sword, for there are no simple assertions. And so it is only poetry that can begin to express it or touch on it. Poetry is the only expression of belief, and only insofar as any such expression can go anyway.

Yet along with Eliot, this also makes possible the otherwise unlikely testimony to the major influence of a sceptical poet. If we take Wallace Stevens literally, the lines in his poem 'Sunday Morning' dismiss the saviour-figure's divinity:

> She hears, upon that water without sound,
> A voice that cries, "The tomb in Palestine
> Is not the porch of spirits lingering.
> It is the grave of Jesus, where he lay."

Thomas's testimony in *No Truce with the Furies,* 'Homage to Wallace Stevens', is uncharacteristically direct:

> I turn now
> not to the Bible
> but to Wallace Stevens...
>
>   Blessings, Stevens;
> I stand with my back to grammar
> at an altar you never aspired
> to, celebrating the sacrament
> of the imagination whose high-priest
> notwithstanding you are.

Stevens's poetic creed was that religious vision had to give way to human imagination in a secular and godless world. But as said earlier, Thomas has credited Stevens before, both in his poetry and out of it. And yet this present collection *No Truce with the Furies* has Thomas carrying on his new, if slight preoccupation with the figure of Christ. That is to say, the homage is not to any beliefs of Stevens, but to his instinctive sense of the meditative saturation of language. The debt to Eliot is the debt of (poetically) working out one's salvation diligently.

But where Thomas's Christ actually figures in the theological scheme of things tentatively outlined above is hard to say. There is a new attention, not just to Christ but to Christmas. 'Blind Noel' has already been cited. In 'The Mass of Christ', a longer and complex poem, Thomas makes the incarnation mysteriously inseparable from a cosmic yet animal sacrifice:

> This day I am with the beasts –
> animal Christmas – staring
> with brute eyes at the mystery
> in the cradle.

In 'Christmas Eve' the heavenly babe "comes to us this midnight/invisible as radiation". In 'Incarnations', though it traverses Christ's whole life, we are asked

> What was the Incarnation
> but the waking dream of one
> calling himself Son of Man?

In 'Symbols' Christ's significance is distended and, whatever his divine status, has capacities beyond the usually mortal: "He was with the future/always, but warning of it,/too... He consented/to be hung up on one/of these same symbols,/knowing that their deployment was/synonymous with the death of the poem." At this late stage in Thomas's own life's work, it is less what Christ means exactly, than that the matter should be thus newly engaged, that is of interest. The poem 'Nativity' in *Mass for Hard Times* anticipated this explicitly yet somewhat sardonically, for on "Christmas Eve! Five/hundred poets waited, pen/poised above paper,/for the poem to arrive,/bells ringing".

Other poems in *No Truce with the Furies* enact and re-enact the Thomas terrain as ever, so essential as a locus of his central meditations. In 'Swallows' the bird's annual migration is compared to the poet's own, yet he still evokes them vividly, perched on the wires of their music's notation. For an extended and subtly metaphysical comparison of the flightless human with the feathered creatures Thomas has so long valued, 'Incubation' is worth citing in full:

> In the absence of such wings
> as were denied us we insist

on inheriting others from the machine.
The eggs that we incubate bring forth
in addition to saints monsters,
the featherless brood whose one thing
in common with dunnocks is
that they do not migrate. We are fascinated
by evil; almost you could say
it is the plumage we acquire
by natural selection. There is a contradiction
here. Generally subdued feathers
in birds are compensated for
by luxuriant song. Not so these
whose frayed notes go with their plain clothes.
It is we who, gaudy as jays,
make cacophonous music under an egg-shell sky.

("Dunnock" is the common sparrow.) The last two lines take us back some fifty years to 'Cynddylan on a Tractor' — but what were then the "bright jays" are now metaphor of our own garish clothes and noises. The owl, too, is directly treated in two poems and metaphor of God in a third, although 'Bestiary' moves into the mammal and reptile kingdoms with equal facility. But how exactly fitting, too, is the change of register into the short sentence, "there is a contradiction /Here". It follows the disturbing idea of evil as our plumage and precedes the authoritative statement about the connection between song and plumage in the genus. That short intervention, as though the poet is caught up sharp by his own thinking, contrasts the more regular Thomas method in poem after poem in these later years – right back indeed to *Laboratories of the Spirit* and earlier. Each terse question or observation stands off the next, or prompts it, or simply precedes it in bare juxtaposition. The key phrases feel as if they were assembled previously and pared down to their metaphorical or assertive essentials. (When this method is formalised it results in the "list" poems such as 'Runes'.) But there are more poems of this kind in *No Truce with the Furies* than in previous collections. Poem after poem is a single paragraph, without dialogue, hesitation or regular formality. As well as 'Incubation' there are the many variations on the general religious meditation: 'Meteorological', 'Heretics', 'Nuance', 'No Jonahs', 'Symbols', 'Circles', 'At The End', 'Mischief', 'Near and Far', 'The Indians and the Elephant', 'Winged God', 'Neither', 'The Promise',

'Bird Watching' and 'Guests'. None has stanza divisions or paragraph breaks. They seem to evince the poet's arrival at a method
that unfolds his crisp, metaphorically self-evoking thought as a
matter now of an even pace he works with great flexibility. It is this
that takes him to the conviction, already suggested, that the search
for tentative expression of the response to God is itself, in the event,
that expression.

One has a sense, in this final collection, of poems being assembled from many origins. They aren't mere leftovers, but have no
need of an overall motif to unite them, as was the case in the previous collections of this final period. The maturation of the writing
means Thomas could assemble a collection from what he had,
because the unifying theme had become his poetic life itself, now
approaching its conclusion. And so we find pieces on younger sexuality and love ('X loves Y' and the entirely beautiful 'Vespers'); on
Wales isolatedly in 'Nant Gwrtheyrn' and more fully in 'The Lost';
and on navigation in the poem of that name, where the poet draws
on childhood memories of Holyhead and his father's occupation as
merchant seaman. Here on this "latest stage/of my journey" he sees
the "storeyed liners" leave the port. These are presumably the top-
heavy commercial ferries of recent years, what Thomas calls the
"thudding substitutes/for the billowing schooners/that were blown
away as though/they were time's clouds". Again an old image is re-
used, but with a lateral shift, this time recalling the "tall clouds" that
"sail westward full-rigged" in the poem 'Enigma', also written nearly
fifty years back. Then, the clouds were compared to ships, while
here it is the reverse. But the ships are not merely compared to but
carried away like the clouds, now with the added dimension of time.
Similarly, although Wales itself is evoked less often explicitly, and
seldom in a full poem, the gently increased citing of the birds of
Rhiannon seems to tie the poet's love of birds into a deep mythology of his own. The independence he needed and fought to attain
for Wales has the singing from that story as its musical heart.
'Afallon' is the prototype poem there.

It is this overall vocational unity in Thomas's whole body of work
that convinces. The sense of a voice larger than life – whatever we
may know biographically – could only be achieved given certain
components. Something is being said or sung for a lifetime; it is
done with authority and power; and such authority is being achieved
before our eyes over decades, by application, observation, controlled

feeling, changes of life-situation, and a germane calling, in this case the priesthood. The whole is also amalgamated with a political belief, a sense of nature, and a sense of people. All of this makes for the yield of poems that continued even when, presumably, powers were beginning to subside.

What then can be said in conclusion, about this poet who has now finished? There is a sense of great restlessness, but in great spaces. The search for the ever-new metaphor, or the stumbling on it unawares, is one aspect of the restlessness. In 'Afallon' in *No Truce with the Furies* for example, the river-metaphors multiply in the old *dyfalu* manner: its "lichened manuscripts/of stone; its wind-laundered/clouds; the moving/staircases of its streams". Even so late the questions take on new complexity and insistence. "Why, then, of all possible/turnings do we take/this one rather than that, /when the only signs discernible/are what no one has erected?" ('The Waiting', same collection). The same restlessness is evinced in the sexuality, the dear wife mourned but old loves also recalled. Here a biographical observation could be striking and hazardous at once. But Thomas's lifelong wife was English, his second wife and widow is a Canadian, one of only two other female dedicatees of a collection French (*Between Here and Now*), and of only two or three more (real or imagined) ever to capture such attention one was the "Mrs Li, whose person I adore" way back in *The Bread of Truth* of 1963. Welsh females figure differently. To attempt personal inference from this would be merely crass; but more generally, there does seem a line drawn between the objects of sexual and spiritual desire, and the political realm where one stands up to fight. Only in that mysterious and captivating myth, of the birds of Rhiannon, do bird, woman and country come together as a sweet glimpse of the unattainable as that can be palpably imagined. Is then the god female, or at least does it have to be flying away, out of reach to be worth attaining, is this what the absent/present god embodies? The imaginative grip of outer space, the stars and receding galaxies, seem to have the same fascination for Thomas as did the empty moor on which the poet went walking cap in hand, also decades back when he was younger. The poem 'The Elusive' (*No Truce with the Furies*) ties the sense of aspiration to that of the female too:

> There must be an exit by which
> she escapes into those unbuilt

> areas of the imagination, where sense
> must give way to thought and thought
> to repining.

The elusive loved woman, the bird in the air, the sight of the mid-night sky from the cottage window, the sheet of blank moor or white snow – these are where the invisible viruses can be eluded, and the invisible god poses the insistent, silent, lifelong questions and demands. Such a mode of work seems unable to be finished by its nature. No doubt when the last Thomas poem has been printed, edited, scrutinized and absorbed into the oeuvre by the ever-growing body of readers, the sense of the endless quest will continue, long after the poet's own finite lifetime reached its own conclusion.

Appendix: Minor Collections

(*Young and Old* 1972, *What is a Welshman?* 1974, *The Way Of It* 1977, *Destinations* 1985, *Welsh Airs* 1987, *Frieze* 1993)

"Minor" is a debatable term but is used in a value-free sense here. Thomas has produced six other collections to date, outside of those discussed in the main body of this book. All six are shorter, often markedly so, than Thomas's usual collections, and they commonly contain many poems reprinted from earlier collections, or have some special provenance, or both.

Young and Old is one of a series by various poets written, according to the publisher, "especially for children". With that in mind one is in for a small shock. Thomas treats his young readers as able to cope with the most uncompromisingly black presentation of things, both the world itself metaphysically and domestic life nearer to hand. Of the sea:

> A child's
> plaything?... Mostly
> it is a stomach, where bones,
> wrecks, continents are digested.
>
> ('The Sea')

Of a little girl (the entire poem):

> And if you ask her
> She has no name;
> But her eyes say,
> Water is cold.
>
> She is three years old
> And willing to kiss;
> But her lips say,
> Apples are sour.
>
> ('Madam')

Revealingly, the conclusion of the poem on his own childhood:

> Years went by;
> I escaped, but never outgrew
> The initial contagion.
>   ('I')

Many of these poems are remarkable. There are not the filled-out probes of Thomas's main books, but in that respect they are particularly approachable, and their lucidity offers a way in for the young reader to Thomas's characteristic mode. Topics include astronauts, adolescent girls, and disillusion with countryside, family life, and the classroom. There is an effective poem about a return-journey drive, largely without main verbs, and that allows the strong meaning of the final phrase; "home on the dot". 'Experiments' can be cited in full, comprising as it does the poet's attitudes to science, his own childhood, and more generally an idea of what he is prepared to offer young people – "children" in fact – as poetry both directly graspable and inescapable in import:

> I was not unhappy
> At school, made something
> Of the lessons over the gold heads
> Of the girls. Love, said
> The letters on
> The blackboard. Love, I wrote down
> In my book.
>
>   There was one room,
> However, that was full of
> Jars, test-tubes
> And wet sinks. Poisonous smells
> Came from it, rumours,
> Reports. The children who
> Worked there had glasses and
> Tall skulls. They were pale and
> Looked as though we were part
> Of a boring experiment.

"Rumours" and "reports" barely need comment. The last line leaves us with the punned boredom deliberately intact.

The simple accessibility of these poems makes them easy for

children to read, but also leaves their bleak import inevitable. It would be interesting to know how much and with what results they have been used in schools. The ideology is clearly that children are not to be protected from the real world, either its local suffering or its deeper wound, as Thomas sees it, at the heart of creation. In a world of total media-saturation it is hard to see how the first could be avoided, and so it might seem important not to dodge the second either, as what children will have to face when they are adults. The symbol of this stark and at times loveless inhumanity is the sea. Proportionately, the sea appears more often than in any other Thomas collection except *The Echoes Return Slow*. 'Young and Old', 'Boatmen', 'Harbour', 'Islandmen', 'Horizons', 'Castaway', 'Seaside' and 'The Sea' all have this element of vast extended water which devours, makes no concessions, yet never deludes unless our foolishness allows it. The collection may be summarized by the last two lines of 'Islandmen', in that its poems too,

> keep to the one
> Fact of the sea, its pitilessness, its beauty.

What Is A Welshman? is a very short sequence of twelve linked poems, and it appeared in the years leading up to the debate and vote on devolution of power to Wales and Scotland. The book is unlike anything else the poet has published. The fresh and golden metaphor is missing, and such figures as there are, including those Thomas has come to make his own, are characteristically repetitive if not stale. One's first impression is of a cynicism as sour as it is depressing.

The poems' titles support this feeling. They are linked to one another, and each is a different answer to the question the book's title asks. 'Somewhere to go for a laugh', 'He lies down to be counted' and 'He agrees with Henry Ford' – presumably that history is bunk – are representative. The final title is 'It hurts him to think'. The miserable atmosphere is enhanced, if that is the word, by Thomas's replacement of metaphor with scatology: "pavements filthy with/dog shit", "Iolo licking his arse/for a doublet" and "my ramshackle aerial/keeps the past's goal/against the balls of tomorrow" (where incidentally we might think the poet had got his codes mixed, if we didn't know of his youthful rugby prowess). All quite standard in today's world of course, but not even this poet's usual

demeanour. The last poem, and therefore the sequence, ends referring to the English language. The poet

> sucked their speech
> in with my mother's
> infected milk, so whatever
> · I throw up now is still theirs.

It isn't all like this. In a number of poems Thomas's more usual tangible references and alert perception make for poems substantial
enough as far as they go. However, even those few are neutralized
by their drear titles, and the only truly positive piece is 'The earth
does its best for him', contrasting the artefacts of museum culture
with the living landscape of Wales itself. Yet we will not make much
of any of this without realising that it is, of course, entirely deliberate, so the question is of how successful it is on those terms. My
feeling is that Thomas had long earned the right to make such an
anti-poetic statement if he felt it was time for it, and that he knew
that he had. The sequence simply does not read like a failed attempt
to challenge by extremity, nor – though this is arguably more likely
– a knowing parody of what he saw all about us. Readers at the time
had to face something even less palatable from the Welsh point of
view; namely, that in those politically fraught times Thomas was not
going to give Wales his real poetry because he thought the Welsh
were not worth it.

The *Way Of It* appeared in 1977, toward the end of the first con-
centratedly theological period and the quest to articulate God
(discussed in chapter 3 above). It contains eighteen poems, none of
which goes over the page. The book also contains a number of
accompanying drawings by Barry Hirst, each of which occupies a
page, although there are not as many drawings as poems. This new
feature may evince Thomas's continuing and now gradually more
expressed interest in painting, and the drawings are interesting; but
the poems I think stand on their own without illustration.

The poems individually are as vivid and economical as those
found elsewhere; yet the book as a whole does not accumulate the
full-bodied thrust of the more central collections. This has its own
results. *The Way Of It* is the way of it; life goes on from day to day,
but here in the eyes of someone whose deepest need, it seems, is to
be unflinching, and who for that very reason has to prise out the
hardest aspects and darkest sides of mortal living, to test himself and

his poetry against them. The first poem, 'Travellers', makes clear
that nothing is going to be conceded:

> We
> see now that the journey is
> without end, and there is no joy
> in the knowledge. Going on, going
> back, standing aside – the alternatives
> are appalling, as in the imagining
> of the lost traveller, what he would
> say to us, if he were here
> now, and how discredited we would find it.

The final poem, 'The Way Of It', is about the poet's wife, and
comes as close to acknowledging his need for others as Thomas per-
mitted himself in that period:

> She is at work
> always, mending the garment
> of our marriage, foraging
> like a bird for something
> to eat. If there are thorns
> in my life, it is she who
> will press her breast to them and sing.

Between these two poems come the bleakness and strain of
'Tears', 'Passenger' and 'In Memory', a poem about Thomas's parents. Yet the marriage, at least, can reach a spiritual unity the more
final for having been hard-won in our mortal state:

> looking beyond
> him... to the
> bright place, where their
> undaunted spirits were already walking.
>   ('Two')

Welsh Airs contains thirty-eight poems, of which twenty-four had
already appeared in collections from the previous three decades or
so. The publisher's blurb describes it as a "nationalist" collection,
and the selection from earlier work makes this explicit enough in the
kind of poems included. They concern the areas of life where one's
nationality becomes voiced, focused, whether over a place under

threat; a meeting with an unwelcome outsider; an economic or cultural issue; or a tribute to an active patriot or cultural icon from the past. And so we find 'Border Blues', 'On Hearing A Welshman Speak', 'Afforestation', 'A Country', 'A Welshman at St James's Park', 'Llanrhaeadr-ym-Mochnant', 'Welcome to Wales', 'Loyalties', indeed most of the usual suspects one might say, and many of which we have mentioned already.

Yet a great poem of Wales like 'Welsh Landscape' is omitted. Nor is there any poem from collections published after 1972, fifteen years before *Welsh Airs* itself was published. Of course this is not to say that some of the previously unpublished poems were not written later. But these later poems may hold the key to the collection. They are gathered with each other at the end. Reading them as a group, one senses a note which 'Welsh Landscape', for all its famous ending about a people "sick with inbreeding", hadn't quite reached. That poem was vibrant, mysterious, with its "cries in the dark at night,/As owls answer the moon,/and thick ambush of shadows". These later poems are blacker. Yet they are miles from the negations of *What is a Welshman?* which, no doubt, Thomas had no need to repeat. They generate some great poetry out of the very mournfulness, pessimism and indeed grief, which the poet came to feel about the final condition of Wales. Here is most of 'A Land':

Death lives in this village, the ambulance plies
                              back and fore,
and they look at it through the eternal downpour
                    of their tears.
                              Who was it found
truth's pebble in the stripling
                    river? No-one believed him.

They have hard hands that money adheres
                    to like the scales
of some hideous disease, so that they grizzle
as it is picked off. And the chapel crouches,
a stone monster, waiting to spring,
waiting with the disinfectant of its language
                              for the bodies rotting with
their unsaid prayers.
                              It is at such times
that they sing, not music
                    so much as the sound of a nation

            rending itself, fierce with all the promise
                    of a beauty that might have been theirs.

There seems no hope any longer, and it is bitterly clear just "who
was it found truth's pebble in the stripling river". The poet who
called himself "no-one" (neb) of course: R.S. Thomas. Yet those
very emotions are embodied in poetry that stands square beside
'Welsh Landscape' even as it includes the imagery of ambulance,
disinfectant and money which in the earlier poem would have been
unthinkable. The dead nation sings "not music" we are told, before
the end then swells into a music of its own as strong as any Thomas
has ever given us. The late group of nationalist poems in *Welsh Airs*
seeks a seriousness, depth and complexity of engagement with the
lost nation as though the poet is giving it his all as a definite commitment at a certain time. There is praise for a Welsh patriot and
writer ('Saunders Lewis') but also for English literature ('The
Cause'). Other supporting poems, although far shorter than 'A
Land', convey aspects of how the predicament has come about, or
been experienced. The visitor from "beyond Offa's Dyke" gets a
cool reception:

            Between you
        and our kitchen the front room
        with our framed casualties

        in your fool wars. Over
        polite tea we hand you
        the iced cake of translation.
        It is not what we mean.
                            ('The Parlour')

The double meaning of "framed" is equally icy. A political betrayal
at the highest level had to be borne but can be recorded:

        Lloyd George, not David,

        William, who in defence
        of what his brother
        had abandoned, made a case
        out of staying at home.
                    ('Dead Worthies')

That family could no more divest themselves of their inheritance by their lawyer status ("made a case") than could the humblest of the peasants. Such poems enable the larger statements of loss and defeat to be heroic in their credibility:

> A rare place, but one identifiable
> with other places where on as deep a sea
> men have clung to the last spars of their language
> and gone down with it, unremembered but uncomplaining.
> ('Drowning')

It is as though Thomas has taken up the challenge again at a later time, with a new recognition. If the present generations can't be roused, then the poet's duty is to rise larger than history, and strike a note of poetic pride in defeat which a future Wales may be able to pick up as its clarion with a new resolution. That may sound rather fervid, but I take it that the final poem, a two-hundred line tribute to the eighteenth-century mystic Ann Griffiths, attempts a statement that could be a recourse for future generations. It is a sometimes awkward poem, but of tremendous resilience; each passage draws us in to recognize further the comprehensiveness of what is being expressed:

> Are the Amens over? Ann (Gymraeg)
> you have gone now but left us with the question
> that has a child's simplicity and a child's depth:
> Does the one who called to you,
>
> when the tree was green, call us
> also, if with changed voice,
> now the leaves have fallen and the boughs
> are of plastic, to the same thing?
> ('Fugue For Ann Griffiths')

Destinations is a short collection, like *The Way Of It* also accompanied by illustrations, this time by Paul Nash. Most of its poems also appear in *Experimenting with an Amen*. The collection *Frieze* will also get only cursory attention here, as it is more than usually a special small-press event, is particularly expensive and is difficult to come by. It was published in Germany by the magazine *Babel* which has done much for R.S. Thomas's reputation in Europe. But its imprint of only five hundred copies includes twenty leatherbound and a hundred hardbound, all signed by the author. It contains almost entirely new poems – about thirty – with the presence of Yeats hovering even more strongly than hitherto. It reminds us again of how one of Thomas's chief mentors himself wrote lasting poetry well into old age. Finally, a useful *Selected Poems 1946-1968* appeared in 1973, and a *Collected Poems* in 1993. The latter might seem hardly a project to be called "minor" on any definition. Yet it hasn't been received with unqualified approval, mainly because of the absence of any introduction, and the sense that anything "collected" (admittedly not "complete") should not omit quite so many poems usually regarded as central. However, this is maybe unduly critical. For many new readers or those not familiar with the whole work, it is surely a handy one-volume asset. No doubt it will be superseded in due course by a truly complete edition.

Bibliography

Poetry by R.S. Thomas

Song at the Year's Turning, Poems 1942-1954, Rupert Hart-Davies 1955
Poetry for Supper, Rupert Hart-Davies 1958
Tares, Rupert Hart-Davies 1961
The Bread of Truth, Rupert Hart-Davies 1963
Pietà, Rupert Hart-Davies 1966
Not That He Brought Flowers, Rupert Hart-Davies 1968
Young and Old, Chatto & Windus 1972
H'm, Macmillan 1972
Selected Poems 1946-1968, MacGibbon/Hart-Davies 1973
What Is A Welshman? Christopher Davies 1974
Laboratories of the Spirit, Macmillan 1975
The Way Of It, Coelfrith Press 1977
Frequencies, Macmillan 1978
Between Here and Now, Macmillan 1981
Later Poems 1972-1982 (including new poems), Macmillan 1983
Ingrowing Thoughts, Poetry Wales Press 1985
Destinations, Celandine Press 1985
Experimenting with an Amen, Macmillan 1986
Welsh Airs, Poetry Wales Press 1987
The Echoes Return Slow, Macmillan 1988
Counterpoint, Bloodaxe 1990
Mass for Hard Times, Bloodaxe 1992
Frieze, Babel (Ammersee, Germany) 1993
Collected Poems, Dent 1993
No Truce with the Furies, Bloodaxe 1995

Prose Writings by R.S. Thomas

Autobiographies, translated by Jason Walford Davies, Orion/Phoenix 1997.
     The key items here are *No-one* (1985) and *A Year in Llyn* (1990)
Selected Prose, edited by Sandra Anstey, Poetry Wales Press 1983
The Penguin Book of Religious Verse, 'Introduction', Penguin 1963
Selected Poems of Edward Thomas, 'Introduction', Faber & Faber 1964
A Choice of George Herbert's Verse, 'Introduction', Faber & Faber 1967
A Choice of Wordsworth's Verse, 'Introduction', Faber & Faber 1971

Critical Studies of R.S. Thomas

Agenda (edited by William Cookson), Special Feature on R.S. Thomas, Vol 32 No 2, 1998.

Sandra Anstey (ed.), *Critical Writings on R.S. Thomas*, Poetry Wales Press 1982, revised, 1992.

Anthony Conran, *The Cost of Strangeness: Essays on the English Poets of Wales*, Gomer Press, 1982.

William V.Davis *Miraculous Simplicity: Essays on R.S. Thomas*, University of Arkansas Press, 1993.

Jason Walford Davies, 'Allusions to Welsh Literature in the Writing of R.S. Thomas' in *Welsh Writing in English* Vol 1, pages 75-127, 1995.

A.E. Dyson, *Yeats, Eliot and R.S. Thomas: Riding the Echo*, Macmillan, 1981.

W. Moelwyn Merchant, *R.S. Thomas*, University of Wales Press for the Welsh Arts Council, 1979

New Welsh Review (edited by Robin Reeves), R.S. Thomas at Eighty (Special Feature), Spring, 1993.

D.Z. Phillips, *R.S. Thomas and the Hidden God*, Macmillan, 1986.

Poetry Wales (edited by Meic Stephens), R.S. Thomas Special Issue, Spring, 1972.

Poetry Wales (edited by J.P. Ward), R.S. Thomas's later poetry Special Feature, Spring, 1979.

Poetry Wales (edited by Richard Poole), R.S. Thomas at Eighty Special Feature, July 1993.

Elaine Shepherd, *R.S. Thomas: Conceding an Absence*, Macmillan, 1996.

M. Wynn Thomas, *The Page's Drift: R.S. Thomas at Eighty*, Seren, 1993.

J.P. Ward, *The Poetry of R.S. Thomas* (first edition) Poetry Wales Press (Seren), 1987

Barbara Prys Williams, 'R.S. Thomas's *The Echoes Return Slow* as autobiography' in *Welsh Writing in English* Vol 2 pages 98-125, 1996.

Justin Wintle, *Furious Interiors: Wales, R.S. Thomas and God*, HarperCollins, 1996.

There have been numerous other individual articles over the years on R.S. Thomas in the journals *The Anglo-Welsh Review, New Welsh Review, Planet* and *Poetry Wales,* and in the yearbook *Welsh Writing in English.*

Selected Related Reading

A.M. Allchin, *Ann Griffiths*, University of Wales Press/Welsh Arts Council, 1976.

Matthew Arnold, *Culture and Anarchy* (edited by J. Dover Wilson), Oxford University Press, 1957.

Peter Atkins, *Creation Revisited*, Penguin Books, 1994.

Augustine, *Confessions* (translated by R.S. Pine-Coffin), Penguin Books, 1961.

Germain Bazin, *Impressionist Paintings in the Louvre*, Thames & Hudson, 1958.

Henri Bergson, *Creative Evolution* (translated by A. Mitchell), Macmillan, 1911.

Max Black, *Models and Metaphors*, Cornell University Press, 1962.

The Cloud of Unknowing (anon) (translated by C.Wolters), Penguin Books, 1961.

Ted Cohen, 'Metaphor and the Cultivation of Intimacy' in *Critical Inquiry*, University of Chicago, Autumn, 1978.

S.T. Coleridge, *The Friend* (edited in 2 vols by Barbara E. Rooke), Routledge & Kegan Paul/Princeton University Press, 1969.

E.T. Davies, *Religion and Society in the Nineteenth Century*, in the series *A New History of Wales* (edited by R.A. Griffiths, K.O. Morgan and J. Beverley Smith), Christopher Davies, 1981.

John Davies, *A History of Wales*, Penguin Books, 1994.

Paul Davies, *God and the New Physics*, Pelican Books, 1984.

Paul Davies, *The Mind of God*, Penguin Books, 1993.

Richard Dawkins, *The Blind Watchmaker*, Longmans, 1986.

Richard Dawkins, *River Out Of Eden*, Orion/Phoenix, 1996.

Daniel C. Dennett, *Consciousness Explained*, Penguin Books, 1993.

Jacques Derrida, *Writing and Difference* (translated by Alan Bass), Routledge & Kegan Paul, 1978.

Jacques Derrida, *Positions* (translated by Alan Bass), Athlone Press, 1981.

C.H. Dodd, *History and the Gospel*, Hodder & Stoughton, 1964.

D.L. Edwards, *A Key to the Old Testament*, Collins, 1976.

T.S. Eliot, *Collected Poems 1909-1962*, Faber & Faber Ltd, 1974.

Northrop Frye, *An Anatomy of Criticism*, Princeton University Press, 1957.

Northrop Frye, *The Great Code: The Bible as Literature*, Ark Paperbacks, 1983.

Joseph L. Graham, *Onomatopoetics: Theory of Language and Literature*, Cambridge University Press, 1992.

Susan Greenfield, *The Private Life of The Brain*, Allen Lane, 2000.

George Herbert, *The English Poems*, (edited by C.A. Patrides), J.M. Dent Ltd, 1974.

John Hick, *God and the Universe of Faiths*, Fount Paperbacks, 1977.

David Jones, *Epoch and Artist*, Faber & Faber Ltd. 1959,

Gwyn Jones (ed.), *The Oxford Book of Welsh Verse in English*, Oxford University Press. 1977.

R.M. Jones, "Anglo-Welsh: More Definitions", *Planet* 16 Feb/Mar, pages 11-23, 1973.

Immanuel Kant, *Critique of Practical Reason* (translated by L.W. Beck), Doubleday Anchor, 1976.

Soren Kierkegaard, *Attack Upon 'Christendom'* (translated by W. Lowrie), Oxford University Press, 1944.

Soren Kierkegaard, *Edifying Discourses* (translated by D. and L. Swenson), Fontana Books, 1958.

Hans Kung, *Does God Exist?* (translated by E. Quinn), Collins, 1980

Sally McFague, *Metaphorical Theology*, SCM Press Ltd, 1983.

Roland Mathias, 'Editorial', in *Anglo-Welsh Review* XIII 31, pages 3-14.

John Milton, *The Complete Poems,* Oxford University Press, 1966.

Prys Morgan, *The Eighteenth Century Renaissance* in the series *A New History of Wales* (edited by R.A. Griffiths, K.O. Morgan and J. Beverley Smith), Christopher Davies, 1981.

Friedrich Nietszche, *Beyond Good and Evil* (translated by R.J. Hollingdale), Penguin Books, 1973.

'On the Narrow Ground of Wales' (anon), *Times Literary Supplement* 1 March, 1974.

D.Z. Phillips, *The Concept of Prayer,* Routledge & Kegan Paul, 1965.

Stanley E. Porter (ed.), *The Nature of Religious Language,* Sheffield Academic Press, 1996.

Herbert Read, *A Concise History of Modern Painting,* Thames & Hudson, 1959.

A.C. Reeves, *The Marcher Lords,* in the series *A New History of Wales* (edited by R.A. Griffiths, K.O. Morgan and J. Beverley Smith), Christopher Davies, 1981.

I.A. Richards, *The Philosophy of Rhetoric,* Oxford University Press, 1936.

Wallace Stevens, *The Collected Poems,* A.A. Knopf Inc, 1954.

Keith Ward, *God, Chance and Necessity,* Oxford: Oneworld Publications, 1996.

Ken Wilber, *A Brief History of Everything,* Gill & Macmillan (Dublin), 1996.

William Wordsworth, *The Poems* (edited in two volumes by John O. Hayden), Penguin Books, 1977.

W.B. Yeats, *Collected Poems,* Macmillan, 1958.

Index to Poems Discussed

(Titles of collections are italicized. Titles in quotation marks signify poems whose title is also that of a painting which is the subject of the poem)

Author Note

John Powell Ward was educated at the Universities of Toronto, Cambridge and Wales. He is an Honorary Research Fellow at the University of Wales, Swansea, where he taught for many years.

His critical works include *Poetry and the Sociological Idea, Wordsworth's Language of Men, Raymond Williams, The English Line* and *As You Like It*. He is also the author of six collections of poetry, including *The Clearing* (Welsh Arts Council Poetry Prize, 1985) and was the editor of *Poetry Wales* from 1975 to 1980. He is currently the editor of the Border Lines series for Seren. He divides his time between Wales and Kent.